degeneration of every field of the arts on full display in what is oxymoronically referred to as modern culture, it is easy to conclude that no new art can be created in such a diseased society. Once and awhile something comes along to disprove this hypothesis (if only with an exception that proves a rule). David Lane's *The Tragedy of King Lewis the Sixteenth* is just such a work."

—**PROFESSOR BRIAN MCCALL**, Orpha and Maurice Merrill Professor at University of Oklahoma College of Law; Editor of *The Catholic Family News*

Dido: The Tragedy of a Woman

"David Lane's verse tragedy *Dido* subtly adapts the classic tale from Virgil to a postmodern clash of culture—a clash between civilized people who honor reason and Natural Law and a barbarous people who give license to passion and demand child sacrifice. This clash is occurring today both globally and within our own borders. I found the play very thought-provoking."

—†**ANNE BARBEAU GARDINER**, former Professor of English literature at John Jay College, CUNY, prolific author of scholarly books and articles

"Dipping into the Western tradition in both subject and form, David Lane in *Dido: The Tragedy of a Woman* weaves another thread into one of the most essential stories in Western Civilization: the tragic love of Dido for the Trojan Aeneas. Mr. Lane's command of the emotional life of his characters is triumphantly polished, at the same time he maintains a finely tuned pathos. In *Dido* Mr. Lane demonstrates a mastery of blank verse, building upon a keen musical sense developed in his equally delightful *Tragedy of King Lewis the Sixteenth*. *Dido: The Tragedy of a Woman* is a rare work of civilized poetry."

—**DR. JESSE RUSSELL**, Ph.D.

"David Lane has done it again. He has resurrected in all its glory, and without affectation, the high yet elegantly simple diction of traditional blank verse to tell a tragic tale from the *Aeneid*. Read *Dido: The Tragedy of a Woman* and you will marvel at, even envy, this achievement."

—**CHRISTOPHER A. FERRARA**, Esq.

The Tragedy of
Orpheus and the Maenads

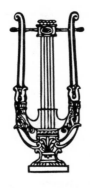

THE TRAGEDY OF
ORPHEUS AND THE MAENADS

&

A YOUNG POET'S ELEGY TO THE COURT OF GOD

DAVID LANE

AROUCA
PRESS

ISBN: 978-1-990685-59-0

Arouca Press
PO Box 55003
Bridgeport PO
Waterloo, ON N2J 3G0
Canada
www.aroucapress.com
Send inquiries to info@aroucapress.com

On the cover:
Nymphs finding the head of Orpheus,
By John William Waterhouse,
1900; private collection.

DEDICATION

Beatae Virgini Mariae Perdolenti.

CONTENTS

ix

PREFACE

AFTER THE EXAMPLE of my two previously published
verse plays, *The Tragedy of King Lewis the Sixteenth* and *Dido*:
The Tragedy of a Woman, I have once more ventured into
the faraway world of poetry, specifically that shining upward
realm of super-rational verities that may be embodied in
story. Again using regular traditional metrics and the tra-
ditional language of poetry, I here present a play calling
forth one of the seminal stories of ancient Greek mythology.
I have enlisted the figure of Orpheus, the preternaturally
great poet who has haunted the imagination of Western
man for millennia, to address in dramatic form the sub-
ject I first treated in my long poem *A Young Poet's Elegy to
the Court of God*. Accordingly, *Orpheus and the Maenads* is
a poetical essay in literary criticism. I have retold the myth
by way of addressing Imagism, the literary revolution that
began with "the men of 1914," who abandoning the ratio-
nal aspect of poetry attempted to communicate subrational
dream states apprehending the infinite, rather than imitate
human action in stories conveying some transcendent (i.e.,
super-rational) truth embodied in the interpersonal doings
of men and women.

The reader approaching *Orpheus and the Maenads* should
understand that it presents a tragic love story not at all
depending on his having a scholar's understanding of Imagism,
though Eliot's *Waste Land* and Joyce's *Ulysses* will be more
or less familiar to him.

Following the play, I present the *Young Poet's Elegy*, in
which some twenty-five years ago I was bold enough (or pre-
sumptuous enough) to set forth a theory of poetry and what I
rather briskly considered deviations from the recommended
path. Hence the *Elegy* is itself a poetical essay in literary
criticism, though in the form of a long discourse addressed
first to the angels and then to Saint Thomas Aquinas. I cri-
tique the three types of Romanticism, (1) that of action (e.g.,
mediaeval romances), (2) that of the intellect (i.e., Mannerism),

and (3) that of feeling (e.g., nineteenth-century Romanticism). Imagism is critiqued, as well as Surrealism and the like. By way of avoiding a possibly dull disquisition, I made the *Elegy* an extended metaphor or allegory involving a journey at sea.

It is upon the foundation of this theory that I based my plays, *The Tragedy of King Lewis the Sixteenth*, *Dido: The Tragedy of a Woman*, and *Orpheus and the Maenads*.

Inditing in the perennial Classic style in these works, I have ever in mind Gilbert Murray's evocative words on this poetic tradition: "The magic of Memory [is] at work . . . the 'waker of longing,' the enchantress who turns the common to the heavenly and fills men's eyes with tears because the things that are now past were so beautiful."

D. L.
New York
May 2023

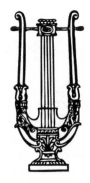

THE TRAGEDY OF
ORPHEUS AND
THE MAENADS

Dramatis Personae

Orpheus, a preternaturally great musician and poet
Apollo, god of music, songs, dance, and poetry
Calliope, mother to Orpheus and muse of epic poetry
Polymnia, sister to Orpheus and muse of divine hymns and
    mimic art
Melpomene, muse of tragedy
Dionysus, god of the vine, leader of the ecstatic maenads
Eurypyle, a maenad
Theope, a maenad
Agave, a maenad, mother to Pentheus, deceased King of Thebes
Eurydice, deceased wife to Orpheus
Tiresias, a blind old soothsayer
Dis, god of the underworld
Eurydice, ghost of Orpheus's wife

ACT I

Scene 1

[*In a dense wood enter Eurypyle, who has been separated from her sister maenads. She wears the skin of a panther, wears a snake on her locks, and bears the thyrsus.*]

EURYPYLE

My mind's amazed as of my reeling way
I make as by a sempster's fixed regard
The best I might through all this wild'ring wood,
Itself a maze. No maenad I unless
My maenads sib surround me, whence we may
Sweet Dion, fairest of the gods, attend
And quaff his bubble-crownèd ecstasies.
How came we parted one from other, what
The drunken crank or twist I took to part
Me from my frantic friends these minutes gone
I cannot guess. Halloo, halloo! Reply,
Who wander wide. O my sistren twain,
Ye come!

THEOPE

[*Making a sweeping gesture.*]
　　　　What less these happy purlieus than
Our home [*She trips.*], though rank and rooted deep as here
They be, where reigns the One with hair envined
And hung with clustered grapes — sweet, shining fonts
Whence we who thirst may draw uncommon drink.

3

AGAVE

Oh, from those purpled orbs may wine be e'er
Exprest and dancing ecstasies extract!

EURYPYLE

I'fegs, hysteric twain, we're much abroad
The mark; we have exorbitated wide
From those exorbitations of the God,
Directly absent whom our raptures fade
And fleet away. Forfend it Jupiter
How he should think us reprobate! The thought
Must put us to the blush. We must e'en now
His shapely prints invent and, nose to ground,
Straight clew them to his godly presence. It
Requires much to have that most exalt
Society of Dionysus, calm
Incendiary of our tripping hearts.
Oh, full as feather-heelèd Mercury
We'll fly to him the ruby drink to take
That reaches up the wetted throat much shrieks
Of joy and feats prodigious, citing nerve
And muscle preternatural in their pow'r,
Misthought of sober city-folk as marks
Of madness. Hence, our company eschews
The cities, frigid in their rounds of rote.
As free we breathe as nymph and fur-haunch faun.
What town could e'er contain our ecstasies
At rage about the land, or wood or mead,
Commodious ground and cordial to our musts?

AGAVE

Then, sweetings, let us hence; but first what shall
These many crimson sprinklings be, I pray,
Upon our snowy weeds of white, as by
Some ruddy wine or blood imbruing. Tell.

THEOPE

[*Falling into a trance.*]
Methinks I see King Pentheus slain and strewn.

4

EURYPYLE

[*In a low voice to Theope.*]
Oh pray, say not this word in shot of our
Agave's ear's oblivion. If she
Should come to know how what but hours agone
We three becharmed did swift dispatch and tear
In bloody pieces was quite other than
The brawnèd bulk and huge of bristling boar
That seemed about to rush upon us with
Its ivory tushes long by gnashing sharped
To slash and flay, but was in dreadful stead
Her father, Pentheus, late King of Thebes,
Who Dionysus self did dare to scorn
And scout, her sanity would soon be crushed
And graved beneath a ground of smoth'ring guilt.

AGAVE

What said'st thou of my father, Theope?

THEOPE

That Pentheus is like the silvern moon,
Reflexion fair of golden Jupiter,
Sapphiric sire of Dionysus blest.

AGAVE

The man whom after blessed Dion I
Have e'er most loved of men, the father of
My heart, of grave and stately port, one full
Of saws and sage advice, who answering
My waywardness, howe'er, would only flap
Me with a fox's tail, well-meaning man
Indeed, whom still I hope to see before
The slow-stepped rounding of the variegate year.
A pity 'tis he likes our Dion not,
Our giver of unbounded joys, whom he
Saw fit to put forever to the ban
Within the spacious reach of Thebes renowned.

5

EURYPYLE

Needs now we must find out and follow him
Who by the clamberskull o' th' grape draws out
The feeling forge of heart and dizzied head
Our ecstasies at caper 'cross the land.

THEOPE

Then, longer let us tarry not, but like
The twilight twittering birds at careless flight
Across the dark'ning sky — exulting trine
Of swallows we — break swift away and wing
To Dion, master of divine misrule.
[*Exeunt.*]

SCENE 2

[*Enter in the same place Orpheus carrying a lyre.*]

ORPHEUS

Eurydice, my lost for aye, I go
Somewhither, where I care not; sure, my self
Soul's inward gates and porches I've made fast
Against the insistent outwardness of town,
Or kith or kin. No embassades from thence
Will I receive — night's sneaking draw-latch nor
No less noon's prying neighbor. These I fly
That better I may sing and weep thee 'midst
This vast surrounding, surd in part, in part
With sense endued, but void of man, save me
And thy remembered self, now lost to Dis
Invincible. My wretchedness I speak
In spirit unto thee. None other ears
I try, though kindred to my tears should hang
Upon these lips. Lo, I shall mourn thee till
My doom. But inches from the brightening verge
Of earth and dazzling day to which we made
Ascent from death, my turn thy beauty's face
To scan was my so grim undoing. Thou
Wast straight pulled downward all without remorse

6

In dun and vap'rous shrouds wrapt round, alack!
That warning word of Death how I must look
Thee not as we upclimbed and clambered I
Forgot, despotic passion speaking out
Of my poor, pounding heart an ardent urge
'Fore which resolve must quickly deliquesce.
　　But now the heav'n-thrown shroud of night floats down
Upon the the dying day, and I must seek
The leafy dell to fleece me warm and coax
Coy sleep with lyric strain mine eyes to close.
Except for drowsy cricket scrapes, the woods
And meads at ev'n are ever still, though, faith,
I've sometimes seemed to hear a jar of faint,
Far voices — cries and shrieks — borne strange upon
The cooling spirits of th' blind night. They mind
Me something the shrieks of Tartarus.
They're liker much but cries of foxes or
Of squabbling weasels. Come, Eurydice.
[*Exit.*]

SCENE 3

[*Into the presence of Apollo enthroned on Mount Parnassus enter
the muses Calliope, Polymnia, and Melpomene.*]

CALLIOPE, POLYMNIA, AND MELPOMENE
We come, great god Apollo, summoned by
The keeper minion of thy living lyre,
On which thy sweeps and nimble touches mount
On high to ravish th' glittering multitudes,
Who thereat shower influence upon
All budding poets, painters, players, those
As well that carve and grave and build and dance.
Upon thy honeyed words we love to feast;
Pray speak thy will divine for us and we
Will gladly eat and do whatso thou wilt.

APOLLO

Ye muses three, dear daughters ours, of all
The Triple Trine the most exalt, we please
To speak of Orpheus, our votary,
Pale demigod of verse and song and first
Of all the bardic race. Alone his lost
Eurydice with lyric glitterance
He richly cloaks and crowns; for lavishing
Of tears upon her tomb, his dazzled eyne
Have made the world around, or living minds
Or deeds, a swimming unreality
By him to blank oblivion consigned.
It stands a poet true to body forth
The deeds of men and scorn t' ingeminate
Mere moods and feelings all as they should stand
More consequent than all the sufferings of
Heroic do and highest destiny,
Those gravest themes and sad, most patient of
The pluckèd wire and deftly driven pen.

CALLIOPE

As thou hast taught, the highest poesy
Must needs within the Polis ever sound
Her music, realm of interacting men,
Whose actions art selects and imitates
That Many shall with time reveal the One.
We wait upon thee.
[*The three muses make a low curtsey.*]

APOLLO

                    Orpheus thinks himself
Alone those woods and fields along, but thwart
His wand'ring way shall one day come unbid
The mad society of drunken god
And raving votaries who, glutting skins
Of wine, become, not cup-shook layabouts,
But energumens of resistless nerve
And iron sinew by the drink divine
In ecstasy imbrued. They loudly voice

8

With darkly purpled lips till now, "We would
How ev'ry wan'dring wight soe'er we meet
Should make him joint with our society
And unto Dion votary be made."
Should Orpheus at hearing which make mock
Or play the pick-brawl, he would surely pull
Upon his wreathèd head calamities.
Unless a man would tempt a dreadful death,
None durst young Dion's arrogated pow'r
Withstand or set his godhead at a pea.
In patient mien and mild confessed this god
On man most terrible revenges wreaks.
We therefore have in will, sweet children, your
Descent from this Parnassus unto that
Embrangling wood, where lyre speaks love forlorn.
There speak him wisdoms as should turn his steps
To kith and kin of town and farm, who, since
His parting, list in vain to hear the tales
Of olden time, of men of high renown
Whose metal is by fire full sorely tried
Of Heav'n and rendered fine. Man craves to know
There's more than shearing soil and scything corn,
Than vend and buy i' the mart. Descend and stoop
Our Orpheus to our will and his avail.

[*Exeunt Calliope, Polymnia, and Melpomene bowing low and backing away as Apollo fades into luminous clouds.*]

9

ACT II

SCENE 1

[*In a different part of the wood enter Orpheus gently playing a lyre.*]

ORPHEUS

Lo, where the wind awakes and chases round
In rings the frighted leaves and pertly finds
And shivers me with strange presentiment.
'Tis strange again how Nature quick—or tree
Or bird or beast—when in its presence I
Am come, should fail, as now, to quieten
That o'er the hours she might attend and lean
To my so lofty singing. Now I spy
Fair maidens three a-falling grandly down
The goldened air. We two, Eurydice,
Shall soon, methinks, by them be visited.

[*Enter Calliope, Polymnia, and Melpomene.*]

MELPOMENE

All hail, great Orpheus! thou who ravishest
The ears and hearts of men and nature! who
The taut-strung wires and gold hast twitched and swept
These happy years unto the thralling of
Thy trancèd hearers ev'ry one, or man
Or beast or tree or rock; thy wondrous pow'rs
Are sovran whither thou shalt walk soe'er.

Thy poet's lips drop down upon the page
Hyblaean honey, and thy chanting seems
The breathèd fragrance of the flow'rs of May,
Which ornaments her wafting airs and mild.

CALLIOPE

No man, dear son, may aught now said gainsay
And not offend fair truth and candour sweet.
But it requires to say thy heart, ill-conned
Of passion, now is cast keel over on
A lone, unpeopled shore and graveled fast
In constant grieving. Tears and threnodies
Thou let'st and ululat'st well yond the bounds
That Penthos, god of grief, has compassed as
A generous gift to man bereft of wife.
Eurydice herself would chide thee out
Of this uncomely moan, become by now
The mere indulgence of a pampered heart.

ORPHEUS

Oh, Mother, say not so. My heart I love
Not; 'tis Eurydice I venerate,
Whose name enounced becomes a knife that bleeds
My heart tumescent with despair. 'Tis true
That men and cities all I have disowned.
From now my love alone is worth to me.

MELPOMENE

To these thy mother's wisdoms do thou show
Thee bendsome, dear to us and sure to lord
Apollo, thine own guide and tutor of
The arts that thou hast lately used amiss.
Eurydice now lies th' eternal thrall
Of Dis. There's nothing for it but for thee
To medicine mild the groaning bed-thrall of
Thy heart and bend again thy steps to Thrace.
Put not thy fellow men indifferently
Away. 'Tis sad thy verses sonorous,
Thy musics dulcet, sole this outward show

About us hears, say rather echoes. Thy
Sole self it is that hears thy sounded thoughts,
So soon as uttered so soon but vapoured clean
Away, the ears of gods above alone
To charm, perhaps exasperate, dear boy.
Take up the ancient colloquy of sin
And sequent suff'ring, and hard strife twixt men,
That unto knowledge and acceptance leads.

ORPHEUS

Thou cit'st me unto imitation — men,
Their deeds and doings, painted to the eye,
A dull and frigid craft to poets fine.
My purpose fair Eurydice to serve
Shall be to sing the ecstasies of my
Deep-wounded heart, much bled and bleeding still,
Whereof the flowing liquor bathes her tomb.
Let me convey the iridescences,
The full phantasmal play, of all my moods,
To man made manifest in outward things,
By my imagination pilfered to
My transcendental purpose: tears for her.

MELPOMENE

Thine oozing heart, thy sorrow-dropping eyes
Thou mayest sing till thou shouldst roop and wheeze,
But thou shalt never men this side of all
Betweedle into regions crabbed and
Obscure — no matter or by lyre or pipe.

ORPHEUS

Must I, Apollo's son, be made thy sport?
And shall my grief be scorned, my art betongued?
My words contemned for skimble-scamble rank?
My heart by thee is cruelly vulned again.
Thou dar'st to hold me up to scorn, as if
I were the bauble of a fool, indeed
A popinjay at which to loose thy darts.

POLYMNIA

Dear brother, sure thy words are silvern tones
Engoldened from thy more-than-mortal lyre.
What less may charmèd ears at list conclude?
'Twas e'vn Apollo self Who hither sent
Us to admonish thee and help, not wound,
Thee more. 'Tis ours to say thou must pursue
That art most worthy of thy gifts by God
Bestowed. Divinest imitation shall
Be just such actions deftly wov'n as will
Create a pattern that once seen as whole
Reveals the unity of life, of one
In many, coming as the dazzling glimpse
Of universal truth that breaks the night
Of ignorance, where myriad haveless men
Recourse to base intoxications of
The moment. Loyally we stand for thee
Be certain, but thy pow'rs were meant for men
Beyond thyself, who crave a meaning clear
And haveable. A lyric must descant
Upon the sense by many shared, who shun
Or stand indifferent to contrivèd shock,
The strange of outward clime. Touch not the wires
As they were verily thy taut-strung nerves.

ORPHEUS

I will not knee before these weary words.
I see thee what thou wouldst for me: a slave
To dullness and aridity. From these
I have untoiled me and will not make soon
Return. Thou tak'st me for a child unborn.

CALLIOPE

Act not the pettigod, my son, and be
Not impious in thy Father's lofty sight.
If everly thy lyre the years along
Thou strike as bard of storied men and gods,
Thou shalt arise the heav'ns to see reward
Amongst the blessed gods, with whom thou'lt throne

13

For aye and by thy earthly brethren be
Much hymned and mirrored for thy passing praise.

ORPHEUS

These words are wounds; I wish them all away.
Ye only would diminishment to me
And hence to her whose heart shall be my tomb.

MELPOMENE

There looms one matter more, young Orpheus,
Whereat the iron-hard resolve thou hast
Just hammered to and clenched may start ere long
And loosen. We must speak a danger to
Thine art, not less thy very person, for
Within these liberties of woods and meads
There goes the new-mint god that lately made
Of grapes such drink as into heads strikes up
And quick to glad the heart — to giddiness
In swallow long, in swallow more to fits
Of madness, finally to lassitude
Of muscles and of mentals. Mark and well,
This god we speak is Dionysus, and
The drink that swills i' the bowl he carries bears
The name of wine, with which much followers
He fetches. Maenads they are called, such fairs
As don the panther's spotted skin and wave
With joy the cone-crowned thyrsus long their god's
Extravagations through the crapulent world,
Wherein each man — from country clod to king —
They have to shrewd recruitment to the grape.
Whene'er they go in drink they have within
The might of Heracles. A drink drunk huge
By madding ones to Dion dedicate
Can spell swift death to one that dares contemn
Their lavished blandishments or stands too nigh
Their revels wild with savage ecstasy.

ORPHEUS

I own how once and again my ears o' nights
Have pricked at what calls forth a vision of
The tortured shades I spied in Tartarus plunged.

CALLIOPE

With hair envined they'll one day fortune stark
Upon thee, Orpheus, past doubt they'll ply
Thine appetites, that they might slave thee head
And heart to their fordrunken Mystagogue.
Sure thou must keep thyself in countenance —
Go gingerly. Thou'rt not a crab enshelled.
Pray speak them fair. Be wise and say to them,
"Such drink as this need not be disallowed,
Which all in measure goes to gladding and
Consoling of the hearts and minds of men."
'Tis sure, their ticements thou wilt frown away,
But of the doing 'tis the manner that
Should worry one that holds thee near her heart.
In fine, dear son, woe worth the day shouldst thou
Incur the maenads' wrath; God help the day
Should they cry harrow on thy head. Thy steps
Turn promptly unto Thebes now lorn, where erst
To all thou warbledst lays of passing joy,
Who till this present pine for thy good rule
And fulgent glories of thy voice and lyre.

ORPHEUS

These haunts and purlieus are beloved home
And hearth to me. My musics charm the pard
And bear, not less the tinèd deer. All trees
Like willows bend and weep; the rocks do melt
And drop fast-falling tears. The humblebees
About my nectared lips oft hover close
To take of poetry's sweet comforting
Or dance above these vibrant wires of gold
To drink sweet diapasons of my woe.
These mighty-given maidens, should they come,
Will liker in the charmèd earshot of

15

My music swoon than breathe seducements vain.
Be sure I shall be safe accoutered in
The silver-woven mail of poetry.

MELPOMENE

Be told as well and warned, not far ago,
Nor far away, was made a murder by
The region maenads of a crownèd king.
'Twas Pentheus did rashly dare the pow'r
Of Dionysus, straight supposing him
An adolescent little-worth, though
To Thebes a threat. The King therein did put
Himself within the danger of the god
And rashly dared his own and royal demise,
Appalling in terrific savagery.
By Dion moved, some sev'ral maenads mad
In drink misthought King Pentheus e'en for
A tusked and sanguinary boar, whereat
With eyes of fire and blood these women wild,
His mother self among the troop (such God
Forfend!), attacked and tore the hapless king
By limb and bloody limb.
                                   Now, be thyself
Not rash when these fair energumens chance
One day upon thine unexpecting self
And song. Give anger no occasion; break
Not into words. The fire-flinger sets
In them a fire that surely turns to leave
The gaping beggar but a shell of ash,
For measure thee with them as e'er thou wilt,
They'll never yield to thee the nodding palm;
But unto them thou'rt like to yield thy life.

ORPHEUS

And should it, dear ones, once misfall me and
These blessed purlieus that these ivied-wands
Should come all wild upon me, should I then
Cry craven? Nay, for constantly I live
Of lamentation. You will find me, hence

16

And ever, soothfast to my dear deceased;
Than this I may not more. Her memory
Is all my food and drink. My songs have from
On high brought down their consolation like
A wisp of birds that flutter feathery fans
As they alight. No, I will not return
To Thrace to sing the dull and saltless tales
Of red, intestine carnage; I shall now
Not listen more. Away as one at once.

POLYMNIA

Be not a cross and angry thwart. 'Twas ev'n
Apollo who dispatched us unto thee;
And we have only brought thee what he said,
And said for what else purpose save thy good?

ORPHEUS

And have you not these minutes set upon
Me rude and birched my back as if I were
A wayward boy? My sword is poetry,
My shield is song, resistless both. The tears
Of panthers start—rough unicorns bend head
And horn to rick their knees—in homage to
My art ineffable. What need have I
For Thrace and all its vulgar merchandry?
Kiss-worthy, sweet Eurydice enchains.

MELPOMENE

Kiss then a phantom, have a ghost to wife,
But well before thou raise the straw-stuck beard
And grizzle, thou shalt know thee for a dunce.

CALLIOPE

Melpomene, let spleen not paint us as
A portrait should be nothing ours. Dear son,
Pray take again thy quarter in thy Thrace,
Where thou wast crowned and kingdomed by myself
And all the multitude of town and tilth,
Lest thou relent thy ghost to maniacs,

Who'll surely set thy musics at a pie's
Heel, nay who in their fervid ecstasies'
Oblivion will nothing hear above
Their shrieks and shrills, who at a trice will show
Them in the role of raving maenad primed
For bloody-minded vengeance. Have a care
And come away with us, if not to Thrace,
Then unto Helicon and Phoebus' throne.

ORPHEUS

Great Genetrix, O mother mine, an it
Were possible here I should stay me by
The space of ever. Know my manner is
To speak all miscreants away, but come
Those bold of whom thou warn'st what may I more
Than find them all with torrent ravishments
Of song? Their madness Phoebus please to mild.
Abide not longer pray, ye three, but go
And to our Phoebus Musagete present
My bounden homage and all gratitudes.

[*Exeunt Calliope, Polymnia, and Melpomene.*]

SCENE 2

[*In the dusk of the same day and in the same place, Orpheus sits
musing by a fire. Presently, he is startled as Eurypyle, Theope,
and Agave stealthily emerge from the shadows. Each wears the
skin of a panther, and a snake around her locks, and bears the
thyrsus. The light from the fire shines upward on their faces,
giving them a sinister appearance.*]

EURYPYLE

Art thou, O man, of whom we three have heard
Report, the poet-king and rhapsodist
Of loss and pain? We spy a harp; we heard
But now a harmony of words and wires
Soft swept that charmed our ruddied ears; we think
'Twas thee. Pathetic monody it was,

18

Full sad, 'tis pity. Dare we reckon how
Thou mightest give us leave to stay thee with
Our help this fading time of weary day?

ORPHEUS

And are ye not a band of whom myself
Have even lately heard: the flinging thralls
Of that divine magician of the grape
That by its mystic juice is much eclipsed?

THEOPE

If thralls, we joy to thrill through woods, up hill
To dash, down dale to roll, abandoning
Ourselves to shrieks and headlong somersets,
But stopping long enough to tear up trees,
Ev'n by their roots, for they were little more
Than cumber-grounds athwart our frantic way.
　　But tell, what helps to thy so sorrowed self
May we extend this gloam that closes round
And rudely steals the office of our eyes?
Although thy cloak be going into holes,
'Twould seem of all thou need'st thou find'st thyself,
Unless thou need a wilder ecstasy.

ORPHEUS

[*Looking skyward.*]
Now conquers Night, whose scepter see above
All crusted round with glitt'ring diamonds
Set wondrous off with yonder glowing pearl!
They silent wheel until Aurora's crown
Of crimson slowly rises radiant
To break Night's sombre reign. With sable cloak
About him cast he swiftly glides away.

AGAVE

How mightily thou say'st and charm'st us with
Thy melting numbers; hearts must soft relent. [*Regarding
　　him narrowly.*]
I deem thou look'st a weary go-to-bed.

May sleep recruit thee for the morrow do.
Till then 'tis ours to find and follow ev'n
That god that calls us out our vapid selves
To drink and transports. Now the heady juice
Will have us into ecstasies from this
To noon, perhaps the night next coming, all
As leads the Mystagogue. And thou, fair boy—
Of Phoebus, image—whose sweet song and form
Have caused our smitten hearts to strike with love,
Must join thee to our rare society
Of Dion. Like to thee, the city cramp
And close we have forsook; though tripping through
The pester of these grounded leaves and sticks
And crambles, we much glad t' extravagate
In sweetest innocency. Sure we seek
No solitude, but sole the company
Of one with other and of all with him,
The god of vines and nectarous honey dropt.

ORPHEUS

Not more need I, ye three, than mourn at long
My lovely, lost to these my needy eyes.
No company I crave except the Lost,
Who looks me sighing through the mists of morn
Or weeping through the showers wept at ev'n.
Our sadness mutual I sing and sob.

EURYPYLE

Make not so long thine hours at moan. A horn
Of boundless plenitude we tender here.
May whatso dreams be carried hither on
The airs of night be few for thee and fair.

[*Exeunt Eurypyle, Theope, and Agave.*]

ORPHEUS

[*Speaking as to Eurydice.*]
And did the music Trine that lately came
To warn and counsel me do so in vain?

This trine of maenads, strange festooned with snakes
With menace hissing, shooting fiercely forth
Their splitten tongues to find a prey to sting
And swallow, showed them wondrous friendly, much
As they might elf my hair and chuck my chin,
But whose o'er-spotted hides of panther did
To me betray frenetic humours. Whence
Beware they rush not on thee, as upon
King Pentheus, late strewn across the lea.
　　　The air now somewhat briskens, as the hour
Of glad down-lying steals and weighs upon
Mine eyes. Along this turf and leaf I'll stretch
And cloak these weary limbs. Come Sleep divine.
[*He sleeps.*]

[*Enter wildly shouting and screaming, Eurypyle, Theope, and
Agave disheveled and madly running to and fro and around
Orpheus jolted awake, their loose panther skins brushing him as
they pass. Exeunt the three running and shouting.*]

ORPHEUS

[*Astonished.*]
Apollo send me quiet mind and peace!
What deeds of evil shall be in their might?
What evils fledged and sharped do not within
Their quivers rattle threats as now? If come
They once again, I'll tauten my resolve;
To them I will not crook the knee, who pricked
Me subtly their athletic band to join.

[*He resumes his night's sleep.*]

ACT III

SCENE 1

[The next morning Orpheus seated chants verse as he plays his lyre.]

ORPHEUS

Alew, no more againward may I go
To thee among the sad, forgotten shades,
But not by me art thou forgot. Of thee
My memory like an eagle sent splits wide
My chest and ranches deep the beating flesh.
The thought of what thou wert and how thou'rt lost
Wrings fervid tribute of my tears, whilst yet
Enmarbling me against mine enemies.

[Enter Tiresias.]

TIRESIAS

Oh ravishments of song! consoling cup
That makes our miseries bearable. How fine
Thy felth of thumb and fingers! Fair thy words,
As they might off old Ajax's shoulders lift
The weight of worlds, though unto men well bred
Thou look'st a ragged jack long out o' doors.

ORPHEUS

Though set in arch and icy clinquant, still
This pearl of praise I take and wear with thanks,
The mounting coolly pitched in the discard.

TIRESIAS

I know thou'rt Orpheus, by men and gods
Well reckoned to the highest reaches of
Parnassus, who didst long and deep imbibe
Th' Pierian waters. Know me for the seer
The blind — Tiresias — who knows thee for
Antagonist to maenads three. Twixt them
And thee there lives, howe'er, a likeness: all
Ye love sensation. Thrills of sadness thou
Wilt chase; 'tis ecstasies 'neath reason they
Will madly drive to ground. Similitude
At sight will urge them unto angling these
Thy purlieus for thy heart's allegiance, that
Similitude may breed affinity.

ORPHEUS

To frowsy fleet-hounds of the tipsy god
An unresponsive, dry-of-milt am I!
I've dragonized the entrance to my heart,
Where burns a flame of consecration to
The Lost. Eurydice, Eurydice,
Return! It was the venomed tooth of asp
About thy creamy ankle winding that
Dispatched thee to the sombre shades of Dis,
Dour god of death. I may not thither go
Again; I bind me to thy memory.

TIRESIAS

Since back to Thrace thou wilt not have thee, where
To weaving story for thy subjects thou
Shouldst selflessly recourse, but wilt the lyre
Embrace for sweeping on the golden nerves
Strung taut by grief, those three bid fiercely fair
To cast thee piecemeal to the midden crows
If thou refuse to join them, who believe
Thee like to them: to feeling fitly spoused.
Play not the rash-brain dunce, but act the sage.
Or wend thee home or join their happy race.

ORPHEUS

And thou, old blathering jackstraw, fitly dare
My patience. Sure I see thee what thou art,
A simple nuisance rudely pushing me
Athissens and athattens, tugging now
Then pushing. Have away this tiresome
Tuition! I shall stem against the wind
Upon this wine-mad sea and not come dead
From being drunken full thereof. To me
The maenads are as naught. And know, old goose,
I'll never bear the stamp of them contempt
For tame and doltish townsmen, bred in Thrace
And unto plough and ledger chained as brutes.

TIRESIAS

And thou, young jackanapes, hast truly shown
Thee pixy-led, who by thy Musagete
Apollo shouldst to pastures green be piped
Lest on a day ev'n as thou sweet-sweet'st thou
Shouldst hear again wild tintamarres of them
That lately paid thee visit; this return
Much more will they be apt to lime thee like
The piping spinks and pipits thou'lt foolishly
Affect. Beware and vex them nothing or
They'll truly teach thee who they are, ask
Apollo else. Do stoutly, man; be not
All lost of wits. To Thrace return this day
Or else throw in—thy runes and notes in tow—
With maenadry. No actions else will save
The integration of thy head and limbs.

ORPHEUS

What need have I to heed the lectures of
A loon? I scarce should be astound if thou
Call'dst cousins with those club-fist amazons.

TIRESIAS

I leave thee to thy madness. Fare thee well.
[*Exit Tiresias.*]

ORPHEUS

Farewell to offal. Out, all sibyls, seers,
And bottle-thralls! 'Tis mine to gainstrive all
These rattlebrains. Crowd now about ye dreams
And memories of sweet Eurydice.
To thee, mine olive, let my lyre speak fair,
My words conjure thy beauty and acclaim.
By love empoppied and o'ercome so soon
As thou didst glimpse upon mine eyes, I've been,
And shall remain, to thee faith-fast and true.

SCENE 2

[*Emerging silently from the trees behind Orpheus enter first
Eurypyle, then Theope and Agave.*]

ORPHEUS

I feel a fan of air that hunts me o'er.

EURYPYLE

We glad again to see thee, Orpheus.
We've given thought how lyric rhapsodies
And lyric lacrimals are cousin one
To other. Thou art something of our band,
For what than sump shall wen more mirror? what
Shall our euphoric wen more near approach
Than thy rhapsodic sump of grief and gloom?
Much patient are we four of feeling: our
Inflation, thy depression — horses hitched,
Oft whipped by crank and quirk and seldom reined.

ORPHEUS

Must I embrace the nomination sump?
Accept my love's devotion as a crank?

EURYPYLE

We see thy sump as digged by thee to hoard
Thy tears, which thou hast diamonded with
Thy wand of poet's wizardry; what more

Dost thou than render thee much woebegone?
Thou'lt better serve thy saddened self if thou
To Dion's glory wilt with harp and tongue
Descant. Sure, wine, sweet bard, is better drink
Than bitter tears. Thus for thy thriving, heed
Our imploration, be thou lief or loath.
Think not our love to scorn lest thou regret.

ORPHEUS

Regret? Pray what shall I regret? I tell
You what I now regret: your presence here,
A thing I nowhat need. Like candle-flies
Ye hover ever round my pestered head.
Sometime like sneaking purse-picks ye approach,
As now; anotherwhen, like elephants
At trumpet, through my gate of solitude
Ye brast, but breaching never this my will
By brick of stout resolve enclosed for aye.
　　That popinjay a-floating like a sponge
Within his cups, who wanders wide and and lures
You into half-wit lunacies, will have
My reverence never. What shall I if not
Like granite weather blowing maniacs?

THEOPE

Trim well thy words lest on the surging ride
Of castigation thou make sudden wrack.
How may a man deny our Dion and
Remain this side the Underworld—indeed
Of Tartarus? At this, two flow'rs to thee
Are haveable: our Dion's smile or death.

ORPHEUS

No doubt can be you stand a savage cross
Of wolf whose cognizance of panther's skin
And crown of odious snake disguises ill
Your fouler quiddities: a whining leash
Of fools—bedraggled trulls and drazels, kin
To momes and loons and lumps. Nor never will

I run your lout in train. Now, get you gone
And whether way ye go it recks me none
So it should be away from me by leagues.

AGAVE

Indeed, no slitless vizard masks thy face;
It shines with candor of a baby's stare,
A gape that late or soon shall freeze till it
Shall desiccate and crumble into dust.
We bid thee fare as one abiding trial.

ORPHEUS

My music shall enmarble me against
Mine enemies. Fare well and far, ye three.

[Exeunt Eurypyle, Theope, and Agave.]

    A world there was once sane and wight, now weak
Become and lost of wits. I wander reft.

[Exit.]

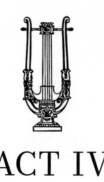

ACT IV

SCENE 1

[*In another place in the countryside, enter Dionysus enthroned in a chariot pulled by bacchanalians. His appearance is that of a handsome youth with clusters of grapes and grape leaves in his hair. Presently enter Eurypyle, Theope, and Agave.*]

DIONYSUS

Now wherefore come so late, my sluggish slows,
Your duty's labours left undone to Us?

EURYPYLE

On wearing miles meseems, well yonder this,
We came to know us lost, through leavy maze
A-wandering till, lo, soft notes of lyre
Our ears did pirate and enravish to
Oblivion. Enchanting words come next
To make oblivion oblivious more,
Were't possible. And Orpheus is the bard.

DIONYSUS

Well known to me, this man, indeed to all
Olympian gods. Apollo's chiefest son,
Twice losing fair Eurydice, his love,
First serpent sting dispatching; his folly own
Then losing her again, so nearly won
By his eclipsing powers. He nothing cares
Till this for other, save the absent ghost,

Eurydice, and sets his tear-stained gloom
Against the comfortable shadow of
His Thracian hearth and throne. What, dear ones, passed
Twixt Orpheus and your far-ambling selves?

THEOPE

We learned, and soon, my lord, his kind is to
Be mulish. Sole his poems, passions on
His bride entombed, shall make his works and days.
He would repose his heart in hers, and not
Besides, as thou hast deigned to say. Wherefore,
We failed t' affriend him; hence, we could not put
Our will upon him, who but seemed at pains
To put the fool upon our thwarted selves.

AGAVE

We made him know his danger: when we asked
Him bluntly whether would he: death or thy
Divinity, he worded us with flout
And obloquy, who only bends himself
Till now how he might better sigh and plain.
And all thy betterness ignoring, he
Headforemost dared thee rudely ridicule.
Forgive the odious jargling of my words,
Surpassing god, but he would have thee for
A good-for-naught. And throwing slander at
Our heads, he brusquely had us three away.
     Those pangs he sounds forth lips and lyre annul
Whate'er revenges rectitude requires
Of us, thy name defending, our probity
Acquitting. Our recourse was sole thine arm.

DIONYSUS

His flow of words sieved clean must tribute make
To our resistless surge of joy, ordained
The world to inundate, on his behoof
Redounding. We will now descend and see
This spoilt original. Short words as his
Have we not heard before? Our fountainous flood

Of transcendental gladness he shall scarce
Refuse and not become a parable.

EURYPYLE
Fair fall thy reign, great god of ours! [*Turning towards the
    bacchanalians.*]   We would
Salute these willing haulsters, pulling aye
With sinew of their lifesome limbs. All hail!

[*Exeunt Dionysus enthroned in this car, pulled by the bacchana-
lians, joined by Eurypyle, Theope, and Agave.*]

SCENE 2
[*In a forest glade enter Orpheus fingering his lyre.*]

ORPHEUS
Eurydice, thine airy name perfumes
This sward, those shining bosks. My heart it stabs
With teen, howe'er, and from these swollen eyes
Cites tears fast down this wan and furrowed face.
Berend my breast no more, but come to me.

[*He sits dejected as Dionysus quietly enters. Orpheus becomes
aware of his presence.*]

I knew not striplings walked these woods. Now in
Thy fooling through these forest ways why must
Thou chance on me? The aliens themselves
Obtruding here come quiet some, as thee;
But I have heard the far-off hollow jar
Of coming tempests, herald of the winds
That drive the rack before it winging and
The drenching falls attending. Many voiced
And fierce they herein enter. "Go afield
And far," I voice to all, not less to thee.
    My spirit's walls are builded stout and at
The corners battled with my stone resolve;
Atop the inward keep I pace and sing.

DIONYSUS

Our lenience but late disdainèd in
Thy fierce vituperation, we have pleased
Withal to bend our wand'rings hitherwards.
How fervid e'er shall be thy fierce dissent,
We ask thy legiance yet. Though blandishments
Gained not upon thee, bend thine angered brows
No more; to alabaster smooth thy front.
How may it serve thy good felicity
To trade that civil sanctimony thou
Revil'st for warbled whine and weeping, voiced
From forth thy founded parapets. Break off
Those sobs of infinite regret! What may
Compare with all the ecstasy expressed
From forth the swelling grape? For naught shall e'er
Be wanting unto one who swashes down
The rubied bowl. And thou wilt flourish, man,
Nor never languish; yea, the trampled press
Gives down our blushing milk fore'er and aye.

ORPHEUS

Is't thou, O Dionysus, vaunted much
By reeling trollops stumbling in thy train?
Pray, know thou'lt not obtain in these attempts
What though the utmost of the tale shall be
Demise. Thy ruby drops are nothing, nor
A purple spoonful I would e'er sup off.
    And must I harken addle heads wound round
With loathly serpent, hated maker of
My passing misery? All hagseeds fly!
Stark barren stay-childs unto drink proclive.
At once and swift, againward go whence thou
Hast come, thou adolescent dandiprat!
I set thee not at little, but at naught.
My airs like wafted venin chase thee hence!

DIONYSUS

Thou'lt see me not again, Dan Orpheus.

31

[*Suddenly about him frisk and gambol panthers, lynxes, and tigers, which may be represented by dancers wearing feline head masks and appropriately coloured tights with paws and tails. Orpheus shows astonishment. Exit Dionysus attended by the creatures.*]

ORPHEUS
[*Addressing Dionysus as if he were present.*]
Thou cam'st to me like whispering surf. Pray if
Again thou mean to come shall I attend
Upon a curling mountain of the main?
     Oh would that thou, Eurydice, might come!

[*Exit dejected and playing the lyre.*]

SCENE 3
[*In the lurid light of the Underworld, enter Dionysus, carrying a goblet. He approaches the throne of Dis, who is taken aback at his approach.*]

DIS
What sirrah, durst thou this my thronedom breach?
[*Regarding him closely.*]
I wonder do I spy thee for the new
Amongst the upper gods, that Dion thrown
From thigh, wast thou? or no, pulled quick, methinks,
From glow of mother's crumbling ash, how say?

DIONYSUS
By Zeus was I begat of Semele,
Whose frail and mortal frame the blinding bolts
Of Zeus's lesser terrors quite consumed,
Divine, unbearable sublimities,
Whose stupefying sight had Hera in
Her jealous hate deceitfully enjoined
My smitten mother to request of Zeus,
Bound fast by oath to grant, though ceded with
A bleak regret. Extract of Zeus I was

And sheltered safe within his thigh, then born
And by the fervid corybants bred up,
Whose love of airy out-of-doors I share.

DIS

Now tell, lord Dion, why shouldst thou of gods
Descend to pay me court? Pray wherefore art
Thou come to me this night perpetual,
By dim asphaltic flames morosely lit?
'Tis sure no man, nor brash divinity,
May casually amble in as he
Were taking th' twittering airs of eventide.

DIONYSUS

I wandered leagues until the birdless mere
I met, whose poison emanations tell
The travel-stained the Underworld is nigh.
A dark mephitic hole I found and dared
The downward jump; thence far and far I fell.
Upon a gloomy ground alit, I stumped
And stumbled till I sudden fetched thy gates
Of iron, where I reached a meaty sop
To savage Cerberus, who seized it brisk
And like a good and greedy dog lay down
And gnawed upon it with the middle of
Its slav'ring treble maws. It little cared
If I or whether man soe'er should wish
To steal his noiseless way within these walks,
But only that its fellow brace of heads
Might make to walk them through its fulsome sop.
    I own that here I'm come, great Monarch of
The dead, to tender thee a betterment.

DIS

And need I, think you, betterment, who rule
This vast demesne of spirits spiritless,
Complaisant to my will whate'er it be?

DIONYSUS

Do on thy magnanimity, I pray,
And deign to me thy sovran ear, that all
The wisdoms I have hived and hither brought
May now succeed from me to thee, and thine.
My purpose, know, is scarce to court thee, but
To render thee such passing joys as they
Should be in spectacle, this gloom at once
Eclipsed and put to flight. In fine, I bring
A drink, a nothing common, one that glads
The burdened heart, the dull and heavy mind.
Empoppied now, now flushed and fired, thou'lt see,
Untoiled of cares, much times of fair delight
If thou this rare and rosy drink pull through
Thy blushing lips and down thy purpled throat.

DIS

Indeed. I spy a leathern skin about
Thee slung, wherein I fancy drink shall be
Reserved, mayhap th' extolled exhilarant.

DIONYSUS

Thine eyes have proved again percipient.
Herein is that elixir, trampled forth
Of grapes and brought by quiet tumult to
Delicious ebullition. Drink, I say,
And be from this a votary of wine,
For thus 'tis styled across the upper world.

DIS

No god shall be a votary; reach here
This vaunted skin.
[*Dionysus hands him the bottle, who thereupon drinks from it.*]
                    I'll now be sworn, young god,
A brook a-stream with rare delights has drenched
This parching palate! Sure, th' Olympian bowl
Of high Olympus here is nigh approached.

34

DIONYSUS

I stand thy friend, great Dis, by doing thee
A good. Such drink speaks well for gods and men.
It shall batoon and stun encroaching cares
And round the dismal world shall tissue gold.
Another pull would do thee better still.

DIS

A noble invitation, to be sure!
[*He drinks again.*]
This smack of gladness I should reckon to
My duties done and well. What god on high
Has so been shunned by mousy men, as I?
Yet, I have ever ruled with rectitude.
My pallor emblems nothing grim, but sole
The want of smiling sun within this dark
Retire. Could I but see the flowers lance
And blush, the blazing rise of day attend!
But I must wear the crown and wave the rod.

DIONYSUS

Of certain truth, thou now hast mastered th' trick
O' the bowl. Make not to swear me down, great god,
But be to me this fleeting while attent.
These murky purlieus through there goes in grief
A nymph thou know'st, as passing fair as sad,
For she had near returned to sun and moon
Above and bliss. Eurydice is she.

DIS

But Dionysus, feckless Orpheus
Had not the self-command to honor my
So wise conditions, but condemned his spouse,
Bereft yet nobly fast of faith, to walk
Again these tracts and trails both grim and drear.

DIONYSUS

This Orpheus, dear Dis, is such a one
As by us brought to join his lyric self

35

To our society must by his voice
And sweeps across the singing nerves and gold
Augment by many times our band. No man
May better win the world to mantling wine.
But toiled at long with pain and seeing still
An infinite regret at losing twice
His bride besainted, liefer would he break
And mud his lyre than sing of ought save fair
Eurydice. His use anight is but
To watch and wish, a-day to weep and word
Sweet wounds of consolation. Nature weeps
With him in soft, relenting euphony.
He throws unmanning song and music at
Intruders all. His sounds have ravished friends
And stringed the sinews of his enemies'
Resolve. To reasoning he proves him deaf.

DIS

And what to me is this conundrum, pray?

DIONYSUS

Great Ruler of the Dead, give up again,
I beg, this flower of the shades, her charms
Restoring unto Orpheus, who then
May sing myself and all those ecstasies
I reach to men and gods. Brim fresh thy bowl.
[*Dis pours and drinks.*]
Frown off thy doubts; sad cares go under! The
Before misfortune that upon his head
Pulled down his all-consuming grief thou hast
The pow'r to nullify—to grant this day
His overwhelming wish to feed once more
His starveling eyes with sight of whom he loves,
The spouses twain arriving sure these tracts
Above to see once more the sun and joy.

DIS

I'm scarce a cold-heart. (This eximious
Elixir softens the granitic head—*heart*.)

Thy boon I herewith grant. Lead forth the nymph
And swift ascend to Orpheus and life
Afresh. [*Addressing a minion.*]
      Have Cerberus the savage stand
At livery and eat not worthies as
They pass. [*Addressing Dionysus.*]
      Leave now whilst yet the flush of drink
Tips wry the crown upon my fuddled head.

DIONYSUS

Fair fall thy reign, O sapient! Give more
Thyself to wine and thou must rule as Zeus.

[*Exit Dionysus. Dis nods in slumber.*]

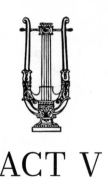

ACT V

SCENE 1

[Enter from a steaming hole in the ground Dionysus with Eurydice.]

DIONYSUS

Hail sun! hail clouds that sail so swiftly off
The wind! Hail zephyrs spiced of th' spreading blooms
Of spring! Our longsome climb at end, I mark
With joy, Eurydice, good wife, thy fog
Of cares evanishes before mine eyes.
Against our going unto Orpheus,
Whose desolation at thy former death
His mind 'fore men and gods has quite deranged,
Take here thy rightful rest, whilst I betake
Me to my fervid minions, whom ere long
I mean for thee to meet. Forthwith all asps
And adders I do wand away; be far
From thee all hurt soe'er. A panther fierce
I'll nearly post to watch lest plunderers
Of probity dare neighborhood to thee.

EURYDICE

My manumission made to me by Dis
I owe to thee. I marvelled how thy suit
He not refused. How potent is such drink
As could his beetling brows unbend! his heart
Of iron exchange for kindly flesh and blood!
    When in my fleeting foot the angry asp

38

Had sunk the poison tooth and sent my shade
To wander in the never-ending gloom
Of Hell, I lower slumped within myself
And, often breaking into tears, I moaned
Amidst my downmost desperation, as
No glimpse of hope shone out to greet mine eyes.
My pangs o'er Orpheus but greatened, for
Our sev'ral thoughts and sentiments had well
Before involved and plaited, making of
Us twain a single heart, a single soul.
Our separation was itself a death.
A wound was opened, staying always fresh.

DIONYSUS

Our swift arise to this thy fresh of life
Revived will be pursued and soon by all
So lasting joys to thee as must the eyes
Of Aphrodite green, whereof this thought
Shall wing my shoon upon the coming road.
I'll tell my lovely sweetlings thou art come;
I'll bring thee how they cherish Orpheus;
Mayhap to thee I'll bring their very selves.
Attend with quiet mind my fleet return.

EURYDICE

Make not long hours, I pray my lord, upon
Thy visitation. How I long to see
My consort! Floods of yearning run more high
With every loitering minute. Take me to
His presence soon; the reach of my desire
Will nowise measure. Gone is dun despair;
The glorious gain of Orpheus is mine!

DIONYSUS

Play quietly, soft airs, through leaves and vines
About and cool this daughter's brow of care.

[*Exit Dionysus. Eurydice sits on a mossy bank, flanked by Italian cypresses.*]

SCENE 2

[In another part of the countryside, enter Dionysus, followed by Eurypyle, Theope, and Agave.]

DIONYSUS

My plans when Orpheus I left were in
The log—unhewn and rough—but now they're planed
And smooth. We must to Queen Eurydice,
Whom I have lately fetched from Dis and death
That she should be restored to Orpheus.
I mean to make her of our happy band,
And 'tis for you to be the fetch-fire to
Her soul, her ligeance winning. Empty of
Instruction, she knows hardly more than child
Unborn, in whose long-scanted soul and gloomed
The sulphurous lamps of Hell shall sudden lose
And vanish in the sun of Orpheus.
At which as maenad newly made she must
Full obviate his dour and stubborn hold
On eremitic solitude. Our goal
Shall be to cite his voice and lyre to our
Essay to win the stolid world to wine.
Ye must, my girls, go with her, inspiriting
Her new resolve to be adherent of
The empyreal bard and spouse regained.

EURYPYLE

To him the fetch-blood we should gladlier be.
We'd give his saucy ship the stem, his harp
To Styx consign. How liefer would we urge
Much suffrages for his deserved demise!

DIONYSUS

Attend my wishes to, ye beauties. Dare
Not bold defiance to your god. Contain
Yourselves and trust my god's sagacity.

THEOPE

O godly being, have sweet patience with
Thy long-abiding votarists. Think not
We love thee less for Orpheus's rude
Affronts. Thy will is ever ours. Command
And watch us do. If Orpheus shall be
Of us, so be it done and soon. Say out,
And we are with thee gone to win this nymph
For gamboling ecstasies, for one so far
Enamoured of Eurydice as he
Could scarce refuse or scorn her blandishments.

DIONYSUS

Then let us forth and find Eurydice,
Speak fair within her ivory ears, and make
Her thump of heart and course of thought our own!
Then shall the man who lifts the poet's voice
And like a magus mad explores the wires
Of gold to thrall the world be ours as well.

SCENE 3

[Returning to Eurydice, enter Dionysus, followed by Eurypyle,
Theope, and Agave. Eurydice rises and approaches them.]

EURYDICE

With all mine eyes I've theeward looked along
These pitted minutes past. What more would I
But hail with thee and these his praise, whose spouse
'Twas mine to be and shall be once again?
These daughters, shall I know them maenads, lord?

DIONYSUS

[Some what abstracted.]
The mass of mortals spelled will haste to him,
And soon, like powdery moths. 'Tis ours to warm
His colded heart. [Recovering himself.]
                    Yes, daughter, maenads three
I cite to thy regard: good Theope,

41

Eurypyle the fair, and much-avouched
Agave. [*Addressing the maenads.*] Greet, ye trine, Eurydice,
Sweet wife of Orpheus, the bard sublime!

THEOPE

How happy that our Master should have brought
Thee forth from Hell and carried thee to us!
We grieve the serpent sting that made thee swound
And sink to earth and death and habiting
With ghostly Dis the grim. The makestrife would
I never prove, but suff'rance grant me, pray,
To state that, if with wine thou wilt thy woes
And worries blunt and with it animate
Thy nerves, thou'lt much the rather joy to fold
Thine Orpheus within thy thirsting arms.

EURYDICE

I startle like a dove surprised; quite dumb
I stand. I nothing need to spur the flanks
Of yen, which stamps the ground e'en now and champs
The steel for bolting unto Orpheus.
What may I do in drink I may not now?

AGAVE

The brimming bowl thy mind will animate.
Our drink thy sweep to Orpheus will speed,
Ev'n like the string by callused fingers drawn—
As it should snap the stave—will speed the bolt
Its mark to find. What time the advent of
Thine ecstasies imbibed he witnesses
He will at once take in the majesty
Of Dion's rule and thenceforth rhapsodize
And drink, so might the wind of words and song
He throws abroad reverb by drink enhanced
And thrill the ages down to Dion's praise,
And to thy spouse's luster scarce the less.

EURYDICE

A mind is his both high and deep of reach;
Perhaps thy wine would lend it reach yet more.

THEOPE

No doubt, thy life below, dear child, was fade
Become, but now I see thee what thou'lt be
When thou hast taken wine and how thou'lt mend
And help his mind whose puissant parts by drink
Recruited shall make new this parching world.
For great account we make of Orpheus;
Let not to me thy pearlèd lugs be deaf.

EURYDICE

When after crowding upwards to this clime
And opened on me dazzling day, to which
By godly guidance I have been conveyed
To you, I little trowed what wondrous friends
Awaited me, but minutes past stuck stiff
And fast within a clay of stark despair.
Full fain and now, I'll drink and then dart fleet
To Orpheus—as swift as dove to cote!

[*Theope fills a bowl from a skin she carries at her side and hands
it to Eurydice, who drinks from it.*]

AGAVE

Thy restoration to thy ne'er-so-true
Shall obviate his long self-banishment
From man's community. What doubt can be
How Orpheus by dint of drinking high
With us and thee and singing highest verse
Will make the myriad world agog and warm
To burn the grains and press the grapes for drink
To honour Dionysus, giver of
Transcendence yond the weary wonts and rote
Of sweat quotidian? The fledgling world
Its fans will spread and wing to golden realms!

43

DIONYSUS

Before the haunts of Orpheus we seek
And search, a caution it requires to say.
We go where risk has used to lurk. Somewhile
From shaggy mountainside descend great boars
That rootle with the snout and hugely feed
On strews of oaken mast. It terrors one
To think how at the sight of hapless man
They bristle as with daggers, gruntle fierce —
White foam about the tuskèd jaws — and glare
With angry blood-red eyen, showing quite
As they were sired by the giant beast
Of Calydon, the largest swine that went.
Fair oft they rush a thew to slash and flay,
The throbbing artery to sever. Pigs
Were pick-quarrels aye. Catch one your scent and you
May after pay with all your bodies' blood.
But be not fooled with fear; let flowing wine
Your mentals school. It stands you much to steel
You with a skin of wine; remain in drink
And you will conquer all and aught that come.
　　　Ere Orpheus should be reduced to skin
And skeleton for mourning thee [*He nods to Eurydice.*];
　　　　　　　　　　　　　lest love's
Devotion thorough absence deliquesce,
Let's take ourselves as feather-heeled to him
Renowned in every clime for poetry,
Whence as by fan of air all go refreshed.

EURYDICE

The drink divine shall triumph in his veins!

[*The maenads and Eurydice each drink from her own wineskin;
with cries of ecstasy exeunt the four pulling the car with Dionysus
enthroned upon it.*]

SCENE 4

[In a glade enter Orpheus holding his lyre.]

ORPHEUS

O sweet my heart, couldst thou but hither now,
Rose-lipped as once thou wert and blessed with skin
Of milken gloss, now tombed and witherèd.
I word and hymn thy sweetness, lost foraye
To creeping envy's bitter venom, oh!
    I seemed but now to hear a faint halloo.
Again it goes, as of a fiercer voice
That loudens with the flying moments of
The coursing sun, as give the gods to hear.
I mind those rude importunates I'd dared
To hope forever gone; pray, let them wend
Away far yonderside the far blue peaks.
    I've wonned and wandered in this wood for lo
These many months, resisting ever with
Vituperation all and divers that
Have dared to tender words of suasion or
The warning word in ear, but let me hence
Make strife no more — do off contentions and
Repent. What can I less, howe'er, than mourn
My loss and moan my life? God help the day!
    At whiles — as now — the tumult louder booms.
Come they that late my tattered patience jobbed
And pecketed, I shall insist upon
My first resolve, without all rancour, beat
They ne'er so much my bended back with yelled
Persuasions, be't such words should ask of me
The full of fortitude — and tolerance.

*[Loud echoing cries are heard. Enter in mad ecstasy Eurypyle,
Theope, Agave, and Eurydice, who, seeing Orpheus, stand in
astonishment. Orpheus recognises Eurydice and, being himself
astonished, obliviously drops his lyre.]*

ORPHEUS

O phantom heart, nay real! thou'rt come to me!
Transformed is now this weary where. Full fill
These eager, empty arms that I might clip
Thee 'gainst my panting heart, ere now come near
Its own quietus since the fangèd writhe
Injected paralytic death within
Thy whitest, lightsome ankle. Hither come!

EURYDICE

Oh, sisters three, oh see! a monster stands
Athwart our careless way, a bristling bulk
That asks an instant action. Tarry not,
But let us four attack as one and pull
The beast apart, lest soon it charge and tusk
From out our thews the scarlet flow of life!

[*Orpheus stands horrified and speechless. Eurypyle, Theope, Agave, and Eurydice raise a furious cry, rush forward, and fall upon Orpheus. At the same time the foliage of trees inhabited by their hamadryads nod forward to obscure the unfolding scene, in which the maenads, including Eurydice, tear Orpheus limb from limb.*]

ORPHEUS

Ay, horrors crowd upon me rank! Alew,
I die! caught fast and jointed ev'n by her
Who ere this present only owned my heart.
[*Addressing Apollo, who along with the muses Calliope, Polymnia, and Melpomene, has appeared above the scene.*]
O Father Loxias, bright Musagete,
Oh would that I thy warning words had ta'en
To this my flutt'ring core, which spills its blood
To speak a vivid dissolution, venge
Of them had named me one of them. My soul
Is setting like the day and netherwards
Must now its miserable mansion find.

EURYDICE

[*Obscured by the trees.*]
By dint of purpled drink the boar is killed!
Now, sisters, fling the gaping monster's head
Upon the boist'rous race of Hebrus' flood.

AGAVE

And therein lave we clean our blooded hands
And arms with gobbets caked. To Dion thence.

[*In a trance, Eurypyle, Theope, Agave, and Eurydice emerge from
the trees. Enter Dionysus from another direction.*]

DIONYSUS

All hail, sectators! Spied ye Orpheus?

[*Eurypyle and Theope speaking each as to herself.*]

EURYPYLE

Its head is not upon it, nor its limbs
Are to its trunk; its blood, a drink for dirt.

THEOPE

Yond lies the beastly body reaved apart—
Shut up in coldest death his shattered bones
And parted limbs—in fine benothinged all.

ORPHEUS

[*Off stage, his head sings as it floats on the River Hebrus.*]
I love thee still, I love thee still, though with
The shadow of a heart that's burst and bled.

EURYDICE

Oh, joy that mocks depiction's laded brush!
My Orpheus returns. Sweet spouse, I come!
[*She turns and runs towards the river, on which she espies
Orpheus's head carried along on the current.*]
Oh gods, ye gods! I quave and faint; the head
We wrenched away was that of Orpheus' self,

47

Whose voice is coming like the surf that swaffs
One sighing surge o'er other. 'Tis the reeds
Reply his soft lament, a music that
Is graving horror 'cross my pounding heart.
[*She walks back to her companions.*]
Yea, still he seems to live, nor longer lies
The swinish cumberworld we thought we left
Him moments gone. I'm vised and visited
By Nemesis; reproach eternal seeks
A nameless sin. It herein sinks like thorn.

AGAVE

Oh, whither went my Pentheus, my son?
When last we walked the grassy Theban lea,
He breathed terrific threats against the god,
E'en him who by and by with sedulous
And oily instigation tempted me
To drink, to all which avid instancy
I offered none resistance, bounding soon
Through woods and fields with friends as ye, sweet trine,
Who palate deep and laugh in lunacy.
    But oh, the monster we dismembered these
Short months agone did seem a boar — one thing
Except: I seemed to hear a piteous cry
Therefrom in accent of my Pentheus —
My Pentheus, dear Pentheus — ye gods,
No boar was there, but only Pentheus!
I killed my son! What horror shall be worse?

EURYPYLE

[*Addressing Dionysus.*]
Have we not here surprised thy true device:
To have to death King Pentheus, as well
This Orpheus, alike thine enemies,
Who honoured, thatched, and fed Agave and
Eurydice, in several, by thee
Made mockeries, who drave them unto shears
And bloody shambles like a run of sheep?

48

DIONYSUS

Mind well your mortal selves new-minted god
Anent. No miserable man, though he
Should be a singer of sublimities,
May gods deny or dare traduce and live.

EURYDICE

I served but meantime in thy blatant band,
Till like a headlong javelin thou shouldst please
To hurl me through his faithful heart; and me
Thou shiveredst, spent and scattered i' the dust.
Both these and I have wandered wood and mead
And made a lark of murder. Sure, thy thirst
Was not for wine, but sole for Orpheus' blood.
My visage roses o'er with shame and guilt.
The ready haulsters of thy car will I
Put far from me and have myself away.
Fall heavy doom upon that wreathèd head.

APOLLO

[*Addressing Dionysus.*]
A lurid canvas of thy cruelties
Are brushed this day, with blood and shrieks distinct.
With purpose but to venge thy pride, thou didst
By sleight of blood-craft foist thy cynic self
Upon an innocent to make of her
Th' unwitting butcher of her spouse, whereby
More exquisite to make his agony.
With help of this fordrunken hatch of dupes
Thou putt'st not wine upon the world, but sole
The giddy staggers of mere drunkenness.
        Think not to stay in drunken league with these
Thy frantic minions, spawning all the world
With maenads more; they must and soon fall full
In fury one on other. Wine pulled deep,
Young god, shall make men murderers or mad.
Thine actions iron answer shall receive:
A soon descension into Tartarus,
Where thou with Ixion and Sisyphus

49

Shalt sport for these thine often deeds and black.
So bitter pains shalt thou endure as shall
Appal Olympus and the world of man.

DIONYSUS
Like thee I reign divine. No bolt this head
May scathe; nor any air this leavy crown
May breathe a-tilt. My smiling Sire, whose thigh
Was womb to me whenas my mother by
His lesser terrors was consumed like flax
By fire caressed, till this has coddled me.

EURYDICE
[*Addressing the absent Orpheus.*]
My love, my love, my sin forgive! I'll go
To him; nor anyone may hinder me.

[*Exit running, followed by Theope, who soon returns walking.*]

THEOPE
The poet's head in arm she sunk beneath
The race to court with him quietus sweet.
If not or falling on a gleaming sword
Or throwing me from off a granite scar,
What can I but think unremitting shame
As I from now weep down a thousand suns?
A shriveled soul stained black and hollow cheeks
With rolling tears stained red are all my meed.

APOLLO
Great ruler of the gods, Zeus Thunderer,
Oh, see thy son, this Dionysus, what
He's late become: with wine and shame uncurbed
He plies the Chloes and Lycaenions —
Such region rustic damsels as may be —
Up steepy elmen woods and down, and 'cross
The sward so green, to sprint at his behest,
Their loosened tresses current i' the wind.
Heads wound with clust'ring grapes, they urge the bowl,

That wine the giddy world should rule. Who dare
Demur tempt stark dismemberment at their
Sanguineous hands. King Pentheus they killed,
As well fair Orpheus, inditer of
Such verse as voiced to nimble sweeps of lyre
Upreared the monuments of human heart
And mind. No matter, he must die the death.
Yet more, he played the bland and monstrous sharp,
Who limed the sweet Eurydice as fast
As pretty thrush to serve as th' innocent
Destroyer of the thing she loved above
All else. This upstart god, an Icarus
That dares our sun, should feel, meseems, the bolt
Upon his insolent and grape-hung head.

ZEUS

Like thee, Apollo, Dionysus is
The cherished issue of Our potent thigh,
But from high thronèd vantage We have mourned
To mark that foul and flagrant deed that made
Eurydice the executioner
Unwitting of the sentence capital.
How may it unrequited go? [*Addressing Dionysus.*] We hurl
A burning bolt upon thine impious head
And cast thee headlong into gaping Hell!
May Tartarus teach thee divinity
Olympian, whereat one dayspring hence
Thou mayst spring up to this thy brother's light
To teach the palate mortal what shall be
Restraint in taking wine to cheer the while
Of wearied life, its endless fits of toil.
[*Amidst a dazzling explosion, Dionysus falls into the abyss.
Zeus ascends to Olympus in majesty.*]

APOLLO

[*Addressing Zeus.*]
Lord Zeus, we put up thanks like incense, as
An odoured, curling pageant that should squire
Thy pompous mount to high Olympus' brow.

[Addressing Agave, Eurypyle, and Theope.]
    No more of carnage rank shall Dion wild
His vanity so foully nourish. Flat
Against the ground of tormens terrible
His shuddering bones are sprawled. Fair Orpheus,
My sad and absent son, what wert thou in
This alien wood, these windy meads, but e'er
The outborn, who forsook thy native hills
And hearth to weep and sing and sing and weep,
Without surcease, for sweet Eurydice?
Be moderate the lyric strain and such
As shall be human; let the subtlety
Of moods deject be nothing morbid and
Be such as may be told and understood.
Suggestion loves to shroud her darkling; much
She lowers at the poet recreant
Would try the cerements of her nemesis,
Bright clarity, she'd keep interred. And through
The winding ways of ev'ry lyrist heart
She breathes her siren's strain, a fluid would
Embalm the bard, to dun opacity
Consigned, and drive the listener away,
By sung and spoken crabbedness repelled.
    In arrogance thou darèd'st say within
Thy heart, "Be banished thought and story both;
Come eremitic image, emblem of
My state of sadness; furl discursion and
The story till I make an image bold—
Alighted from the plodding nag of thought—
Whose import grave the hearer must infer
Or be assigned to vulgar regions of
The dim eclipse of mind." Didst thou persist
Thou hadst strapped tight communication's tongue.

CALLIOPE

Oh Orpheus, my son, when from thy crown
And city thou mad'st brash to sever thee
And purpose unto these stark purlieus, thou
Couldst only make thee prey to them that quite

Transcended thine estrangement. Here thou livedst
At long till lurking madness crept upon
Thee and attendant murder seized thy limbs.
At first the maenads three, for thou wouldst not
Pay heed to their desires, would make about
Thy laurel-crownèd ears a fearsome war
Of roaring menace; soon with faces rosed
Of wine and indignation, they would touse
Thee like a doll and from thy torso pull
Thy legs and arms, as well thy wreathèd head.
   'Tis not, dear son, in genuflection to
The Many—keeping all the fineless world
Of felt and seen peculiarities
In sorry sunder, making life a mere
Adventure of the nerves—shall Truth bud forth,
But sole in fair obeisance to the One,
Which gazes constant through the wafted veil
And dapple of the Many—i' th' metal proved
Of interacting men by danger tried,
Or in the Polis thronged or in the wild.
The One shall be the soul unseen of all
That animates this various world and vast.

APOLLO

In essence, Nature rank and riotous,
Sweet souls, should so be trimmed and comelied as
Her hidden truth and purpose should emerge
And teach poor men at pains to live from day
To harried day what shall their hearts conduct
To gladness, virtue, and a quiet mind.

EURYPYLE

Meseems that 'neath the blood-dark bowl there sweeps
Malignant e'en the dragon drunkenness,
Which leaping down the inwards of a man
Excites to reeling inebriety.
There needs a pow'r to answer peccancy.

THEOPE

It shall be needs the God of lights far yond
Olympian air and orbits. Fetch we down
His care by pious suppliance, He shall
All answerable aid speak instant out
To salve and save the wounded world and raw.
Pray let us make from now our wiser way,
That every wight we chance upon our tale
Of tears we'll sing and sweep the quav'ring wires
And gold across. How can we else, dear sibs?

AGAVE

Oh, I will tell this tristful tale abroad
My filicidal crime to expiate.

[*Exeunt Eurypyle and Theope, oxtering Agave along. Exeunt fading back into clouds Apollo, Calliope, Polymnia, and Melpomene.*]

THE END.

GLOSSARY

Agone:	ago
Alew:	a cry of despair; in hunting, a cry to urge on the pursuers
Againward:	back again
An:	if
Anent:	fronting, close to
Answerable:	suitable, fitting
Attent:	attentive
Athissens *and athattens*:	in this way and that way
At list:	listening, being attentive
Aye:	ever
Batoon:	to cudgel, strike with a baton
Bed-thrall:	a bedridden person
Bendsome:	flexible
Berend:	to rend or tear badly
Betongue:	to assail with the tongue, flout
Betterment:	an improvement, an amelioration
Betweedle:	to entice excessively by music
Blood-craft:	murderous plotting
Bosk:	a small thicket of bushes
Brast:	burst
Call cousins:	to address each other as cousin
Cerements:	grave-clothes, waxed wrappings for the dead
Cite:	to summon
Clamberskull:	strong drink
Clew:	to track as by a clew
Clinquant:	tinsel, false glitter
Cognizance:	a badge, an emblem, or a token
Conn:	to direct the steering of (a ship)
Corybants:	wild attendants of the goddess Cybele, goddess of nature and fertility
Cote:	a dovecote
Crambles:	boughs or branches of crooked growth
Cry craven:	to surrender
Crank:	a bend, a crooked path; a whimsical notion
Crowd:	to force one's way through a confined space
Cry harrow:	to denounce (a person's) doings

Cumber-ground:	a thing (or person) that uselessly cumbers the ground
Cumberworld:	a thing (or person) that uselessly cumbers the world
Cup-shook:	drunken
Current:	flowing
Dandiprat:	a small boy, an insignificant person
Darkling:	in the dark, in darkness
Dayspring:	dawn
Demesne:	a realm, domain
Dion:	Dionysus
Distinct:	decorated, adorned
Dragonize:	to keep guard over as a dragon
Draw-latch:	a sneaking thief
Drazel:	a slut
Elf:	to twist (the hair) as an elf might do
Elmen:	consisting of elm trees
Embrangle:	to entangle, embroil
Empyreal:	celestial, sublime
Endue:	to endow, clothe
Energumen:	a fanatic or zealot; a demoniac
Enounce:	to pronounce
Envine:	to adorn with vines
Eremitic:	pertaining to an eremite or hermit
Everly:	always
Exorbitate:	to stray
Express:	to squeeze, press out
Extract:	extracted
Extravagate:	to roam at will
Eyen:	eyes
Eyne:	eyes
Fade:	insipid, uninteresting
Fair:	a woman
Fans:	wings
Feather-heeled:	having winged heels
Felth:	the power of feeling in the fingers
Fetch-blood:	one who draws blood
Fetch-fire:	one who fetches or lights a fire
Find:	to furnish, supply
Fineless:	infinite, unlimited

Fledge:	to feather (an arrow)
Fool:	to be made foolish
Fordrunken:	overcome with drink
Forfend:	to forbid
Fortune upon:	to happen upon
Front:	forehead
Fulgent:	resplendent. glittering
Gainstrive:	to strive against
Give the stem:	to ram (a ship)
Gloam:	gloaming, twilight
Grave:	to inter
Green:	to make or become jealous
Hagseed:	the offspring of a hag.
Haulster:	one who hauls
Headforemost:	headlong
Hive:	to store up, accumulate
I'fegs:	a trivial oath: in faith, by my faith
Imbrue:	to imbue, stain
Inditer:	a writer, composer
Ingeminate:	to reiterate
Invent:	to find
Jargling:	harsh or discordant sound
Job:	to prod, peck
Joint:	to separate (meat) at the joints
Kind:	nature, natural disposition
Lea:	grass-land
Legiance:	allegiance
Let (tears):	to weep
Liefer:	more willingly
Lief or loath:	willing or unwilling
Like:	to resemble
Liker:	more likely
Lime:	to catch with birdlime
List:	to listen, listen to
Long:	along
Lorn:	forlorn
Lose:	to become deprived of power or force

Loxias:	an epithet of Apollo
Lug:	an ear
Make:	to constitute
Mast:	the fruit of forest trees (e.g., acorns) eaten by wild pigs
Meed:	recompense
Mentals:	intellectual faculties
Mephitic:	foul-smelling, pestilential
Midden:	a dunghill or pile of refuse
Mind:	to remember, think of
Misfall:	to happen unfortunately
Misthought:	mistaken
Mome:	a blockhead, a dolt
Mud:	to cast into the mud
Murrain:	a plague
Musagete:	epithet of Apollo as leader of the Muses
Music:	of or pertaining to the Muses
Musts:	needs
Mystagogue:	one who introduces to religious mysteries
Original:	a odd or curious person
Outborn:	foreigner
Palate:	to gratify the palate, relish
Pard:	a leopard
Passing:	surpassing
Patient of:	susceptible of
Pecket:	to peck repeatedly
Pettigod:	an inferior deity
Pipit:	a songbird with a short and feeble note
Plain:	to complain
Praise:	merit
Prints:	footprints
Proclive:	prone
Puissant:	powerful
Purlieus:	a place that one frequents, environs
Pursue:	to follow, come after in time
Quave:	to quaver, tremble
Quiddity:	an essence, a quality
Quietus:	release from life

Race:	a swift current of water
Rack:	a mass of cloud driven before the wind
Ranch:	to scratch or wound deeply with a sword or an animal's claws
Reaved:	rent, torn
Reft:	bereft
Reck:	to concern or trouble (one)
Recruit:	to refresh, re-invigorate
Rick:	to sprain, twist, wrench
Ride:	a surging motion
Roop:	to utter a hoarse sound
Rootle:	to root
Rote:	habit, mere routine
Rune:	a song, a poem, or a verse
Sapphiric:	of or pertaining to sapphire
Scar:	a cliff
Scout:	to reject with contempt
Sectator:	the follower of a sect
Sempster:	a tailor
Shoon:	shoes
Shrill:	a shrill cry
Sib:	a sister; sisterly
Sistren:	sisters
Skimble-scamble:	confused or worthless discourse
Soothfast:	faithful, loyal
Spink:	a finch
Start:	to become loosened
Start:	to spring forth
Stay:	*refl.* to abide (in a place)
Stay:	to support
Stay-child:	a childless woman
Stem:	a ship's prow
Stoop:	to cause to bow down, subdue
Strike:	to pulsate, throb
Suasory:	persuasive
Suffrages:	intercessory prayers
Surcease:	temporary cessation, suspension
Surd:	insensate
Swaff:	to come one over another, like waves upon a shore
Sward:	grass
Swear down:	to put down by swearing
Sweet-sweet:	to chirp like a bird

Swill:	to move about as liquid in a vessel
Swoond:	to swoon
Teen:	grief, misery
Thorough:	through
Threnody:	a song of lamentation
Thrill:	to pass with a thrill
Thwart:	an ill-tempered or cross person
Ticement:	an enticement
Tilth:	land that has been tilled
Tine:	a pointed branch of a deer's antler
Tintamarre:	uproar, clamour
Tormens:	torments
Torrent:	rushing like a torrent
Touse:	to pull roughly about, worry
Trick:	the art of doing something skillfully or successfully
Trine:	a group of three
Triple Trine:	the nine muses
Tristful:	sorrowful, gloomy
Trow:	to think, suppose
Tush:	a tusk
Ululate:	to lament loudly
Venge:	to avenge
Venge:	vengeance
Venin:	venom
Vizard:	a mask
Vuln:	to wound
Wand away:	to banish as by a magic wand
Whether:	which
Wight:	a human being
Wight:	strong and brave
Wild'ring:	bewildering
Wisp:	a flock (of birds)
Won:	to dwell
Wonts:	customs, habits
Yond:	beyond

A Young Poet's
Elegy to the
Court of God

Part the First

Ye blessed gods created and sublimed
Of God, ye suns who far out-throng the flue
Of winding stars borne round upon the breathed,
Irrefragable Word, ye swiftly bear
Us frailties His gracious errands; and like
Alcyone alit upon the spelled,
Obedient flood of death ye brood the clutch
Of riping souls with feathered panoplies
Of musky wings becrimsoned deep and fair
As th' ruffled rose. The while — oh mystery!
Ye shelter far aloft the glittering vaults
Of night to worship fixed as golden bees
In amber or rapt as the sovran bird that lifts
By noon to the fresh, annunciating winds
And glances undestroyed the flames and beams
Of th' ramping sun (though other eyes and proud
Were mazed and, like Semele entoiled, struck bolt
In ashes). Oh, attend mine instant pray'rs,
Ye interceding angels, especially thou,
Mine Angel Guardian; for, except your love
With orant flame alight shall magnify
My poor beseechments unto God, they must
I' th' white, exceeding brilliancy of Heav'n
Soon faint and 'clipse.
    Atop youth's ridge, upon that headland scar
That fronts the tide of ev'ry wending wight's
Majority, I stand a poet born,
A staved and girded pilgrim hitherwards
Attaining from my native close, where first

I pulled the milk of mercy and delight:
My perdurable Catholic faith and all
The living wonts and uses quick it there
Has incarnated time all out of mind.
Below me now I gaze the sighing surf,
Whose fingers smoothe the beaten sand and draw
The shipmen to her. Like the bards, or great
Or small, that have preceded me and dared
The shrug of Ocean, I must soon embark
And, making sail upon the flood, run straight
For Parnasse and the font of Castaly.
        I cry upon your sanctitudes to stand
The patrons of my humble pen, for ye
Lay hold upon this various world at once
By always very intuitions, which
Themselves as swiftly rapture you. As soon
As thriven bees in rose-bloom ye cast mature
From out the Mind of God, ye cataphracts
As bright as living steel. For ye were not
As who in gentle arm lie hard at suck
And staring on their mindful mothers' eyes.
Nor o'er ye spirits inextense did time
Bear sway, whose pointing tipstaff monishes
Us flesh with fretful taps and larums shrill
How we will dote upon the drowsy charms
Of indolence. Nor yet were ye become
A blighted purlieu to the hob of death,
The sneering, brute familiar that swags
The flesh and fuddles the mind until at glint
Of folding star he shears the lifestrings through
And, being jaded, casts his broken toys
Upon the sleeping dust. But though our souls
Be still at war with self and Hell and, so,
Must offer frequent battle—sometime close
With hideous shape in passage fierce of arms—
'Tis not of grim testudo or the fell
Goliath we are threated—our enemies
All met in reeking, undivided sum
And making boldly at us all at once.

And are we wounded in a sore attempt
And collied, indeed are rived and fall'n amidst
Our ruddy spilth of life, we make our shrift
In tears and rise God's paladins, once more
By grace to stand Hell's blatant emp'ry at
Defiance. But on your own trial's battlestead
How brief your sojourn, yet how hard withal!
To bear salvation's palm all ye must wage
Each one his sword of grace against his own
Armipotent and self-sufficient wraith
And shend him with one stroke or lose the day
And day eternal—in plain, must unto God
All utterly and instantly commend
Yourselves or from His proffered graces shrink
Indign and cold, endungeoning yourselves
Within the oubliette of self for ay.
 So at your thronging forth, th' Almighty God
At once enshrouded ye within the grey
Sequester of a swaddling cloud; for did
Ye front the glory of your sudden God,
Ye must, unwilled and meritless, have drawn
To Him annihilate, like iron crumbles
Twitched dumb to th' imperious magnet. Unto you
Free will He gave and now would prove your faith,
Who whisperèd ye thus: "Our firstlings paled,
Whose self-adverting eyen survey and take
Your inward deeps suspense with all the types
Of Our creation, yield your majesties
To Us, the fiery vast of love, Who will
Not mete, how far soe'er your heated hearts
May urge therein their coltish way and pure.
Come unto Us now rathe and with a will
And rest within Our circling fathom still."
 What tided now, alas, could show no more
To frighted mortal stare than summer's bluff
And elemental greenman, what virid storm
Rebukes aloud the panic vales and strings
Against the sweeping winds a jagged warp
Of fire. For straight upon these words of grace,

There pealed from angel hearts such rhapsody
Of multitudinous praise as here upon
This puisne earth had ravished Typhon from
His wits and made Briareus' heart strike wild.
Then into Heaven ye were haled as flights
And headlong tides of sheeting flame, such fire
As earthly dread might take for levin swords
Wherewith the Lord must hew in shreds the pearled
And diamonded stole of night, or else
For glowing trees wherewith He fain would blind
The single eye of cyclopean day.
To sainted eyes and ears initiate these
High prodigies, wherein of tried ye were
Become triumphant, sure had been those things
They were: th' eternal liturgy of Heav'n
And blaze of your transfiguration. They
Had drawn the blameless, prisoned soul on earth
As if she were the powdered moth of May
That nightlong watching i' the closet's dim
Shall mad against the panes and lattices
Serenely lighted of the fulling moon.
    Not ev'ry angel was advanced above
His natural rise; for, ere your Hold and Hearth
Thus triced you into Heaven, frigid pride,
Your brethren meanly grand and failing shame,
Of Love Divine thought quiet scorn and like
The whisperous wind that ere the tempest rage
Will hunt the trees their crowding, signal leaves
To whelm, they lipped, each one, "I will not serve."
Whom God All Just thereat disprinced and to
The thirsting mouth of Hell at once threw down
Like slant and thunderbolted torrents. Thence
He first in pride, the blackened webster of
A thousand wiles, would sway our parents first
Create and then dispatch amongst their seed
All his dark inclining, who each, against
The universal doom be trumped, must lure
His chase to fool its little span of life
Away and thus to suffer inward rot.

And like the maculate beast that stirs what time
The sun lies bleeding on the western hills,
Each fiend at liberty amongst the stiff
And grinning swath of scything death shall nose
The air for ghostly carrion until
With bloody jaws and sagging belly he
Shall last at Dawn away. Defend us, God!
     But like a mighty air, the Paraclete
Dispersed th' occulting mists, which hurled as hush
And swift away as rack at tempest's end.
And thus th' Almighty God in countenance
Of unconcealèd fire and radiant
The reach of Heaven's aery climates now
Was pleased to luminate, to Whom ye quired
Your everlasting hymn like them that wide
Away in copse and meadow rise from brier
And trailing weed to thrill in stabs of bliss
Their morning canticles of praise unto
The fecundating sun. And from the siege
Of holy radiance the Triune God
Decreed the many-marbled world, all which
Upon ye angels peered in stroke of fly's
Wing, clean from nought both floor of earth and vault
Of sable sky, which after blazoning
With hue of azure day He bossed and swagged
With silver stars and glowing galaxies.
Within this glittering flood of time and space,
A vastity that unto God must like
Unto a solid moment scarcely more
Of bulk than sprite's incorporeity,
All living things should thence by slow degrees
And measurable goings or stand upon
A course for home or fetch away to wrack.
Behold, ye dreadless Host! by God ordained
To governors, shields, and sentinels, at His
Cathedral charge ye lively drave abroad
The universe to wind the galaxies
In great siderial roundelays of laud.
But soft! Forgive these feeble numbers; here

A poet's fancy must to man's five wits
Less rudely character profundity.
These eyes, by Thomas schooled, have late descried
Of your so careful tasks, the awful kind,
Which now my love begs suff 'rance to rehearse.
Whenas the Lord upon a moment thought
Ye into being, He willed of passing love
That, since ye would anon by grace approve
Yourselves His children, all ye should have part
In His creative facts to come. And thus
He found ye full with all th' ideas of
The myriad universe yet uncreate,
Each lapped as tight as winter bud against
Such providential hour as it should quite
Disclose itself to the bare advertence of
Your ardent gaze and blow within your pied
Academies of perfect lore. So soon
As ye their fastness glance to flower by one
And sundry through the while of time, so soon
Their answerable beings show i' the void
Like fairy rings upon the green, as if
Ye breathed from blows immortal tufted crops
Of seed upon a wild and raised therefrom
A brief display of thurible flow'rs to cense
The courts of gold and silver light. At once
In foal new thrown nor licked ye contemplate
The crumping, belted horse; in strew of mast
The stand of oak in all detail ye scry.
And by such intuitions real as fair,
And in the Lord's creative thought subsumed,
Ye still breed up His creatures animate,
Wherewith the fleshed and foliated world
Ye swarm anew. In doings thus exalt
Are limned your more than tutelary pow'rs
Of God our Lord all generous conferred.
    In midst the new-struck fires that stately foot
Their pavans cross the upward night, the earth
Entire must now a swung incensory
Become and breathe to its Creator fumes

68

Of all the grains and gums of life. Upon
Its min'ral ground of hunched and splitten rock
Involving inchmeal o'er a hectic melt
Th' Omnipotent His handiwork fulfilled
By step and step twixt patient being and
Your legion selves, who yet at once were made
More divers far than all through land and sea
Should teem and tribe. At first, and as alway
With your partaking charactered e'vn now,
He formed the merely vital beings, who
To magnify their Gardener but grope
The yielding clods and bush to the cordial sun.
Thereon, He fashioned beings sensitive
And vital both, who in miaul, chirp, blate,
Or squeal their Lord unthought will brutely praise.
    Now waxing much of expectation's warmth,
Ye mantled o'er with charitable joy;
For that ye knew of God that He would soon
The parent of the thrice-ensoulèd race
Of men create, whose inches forth the slime
Of earth He promptly spoke. And having strung
The bones with brawn, and shaped a folden brain,
He thereunto inspired a viewless ghost,
A ghost needs rational; for e'vn as all
Ye unembodied spirits shall be full
Intuitive, so spirits into gross
Extension breathed must unto discourse set
Their lab'ring pow'rs that they may come to know
And thenceforth love and serve their God. Within
This robe of clay the senses thorough time
But victual each the puzzling wits of men
With incremental crusts of sensibles,
Who therewithal must ever fetch and try
Conclusions, which we pray full just may stand.
Now wrenching forth our eldest patriarch
A ruddy rib, th' Almighty God shaped out
Thereof the mother of our race and did
Our parents twain to know His holy Will—
How they should quite abstain their lips from fruit

Of the inviolable tree and thus
Receive eternity of joy at gaze
Upon His beatific Face. Alas,
The Sire of Lies had parted, but not 'scaped,
His everlasting dog-hole and, afoot
Upon the earth, would speak our parents fair
And breathe upon their burnished souls; for sight
Of simple-hearted innocence so greened
His sober gravity as he must snarl
This happy world and swear it of the courts
Of Hell. While yet he curled like kindling in
The roar of Hell's own writhing flames, he coiled
Him into serpent's form and, lancing oft
His cloven tongue the tremulous air to prove,
He nigh our mother drew his odious shape.
With addle heart, but hatching mind, he speaks
Her fair and has, an she but taste of the
Innominable fruit, how she must rise
A goddess, knowing good and ill, and paints
Unto her prompt imagination all
The vanities that since have cozened us,
Her numb'rous strain. At length, come stupid with
The fumes of flattery and sadly flush
With visions of her deity, she could
Not find her pow'r of will; whereon she culled
And tasted. Nor our father better fared.
Albe his spouse's guilt had put him to
A momentary stand, he also, at
Her eager suasion, fleshed his appetite
And on his flagrant head and progeny
Plucked death and ev'ry evil else that here
Lays scourge cross human soul and body. Thus
So far ago the universal mar
Was wrought. Instead of drawing skyward in
Apotheosis, our wretched parents were
Bedwarfed in wringing cramps of guilt and shame.
    But though proudblooded Lucifer and's toads
Acrouch had at their own depravities
Been into lava briskly poled, the Lord

Vouchsafed to spare our parents fall'n. Perchance
They misdemeaned something backward of
Consent or somehow failed to seize of what
They did the deadly gravity. In fine,
Perhaps their being in the flesh was why
All Mercy deigned betimes to grant them and
Their offspring place and long occasion yet
To ripen through His grace for life eterne.
And so against the swoop of the ringing scythe,
Alike the corn and cockle swell within
God's croft of mortal men. But ere killed hearts
Abroad the world might life unhoped obtain
Within His love, th' immeasurable due
Of expiation must be rendered. Thus,
To ev'ry man should ever live He vouched
A Saviour in His only Son begot,
Who came far other than the conqueror
The Chosen waited. For to quit our souls
Of ev'ry chain and iron hamper and
To everlasting peace redeem us home,
He suffered the indignant world to do
Him unto death upon a gallows tree.
Though long since risen from the jealous grave,
He yet stays clenched to this our very tree
Of knowledge and, in this meek attitude,
Descends the suppliant morn to be the Bread
Of our redemption; as well His Sacred Heart
Afire upon the altar urges forth
His Wounds the oozing, infinite measure of
His Blood, our Drink of ever-during life.

  O Jesu, grant that as St. George I might
Each day address my heart in tabard white
Emblazed with sign of those two boards across
And soaken red with Thy most precious Blood
And that sustained of Thy sweet Sacrament
Might rive the monsters on my way to Thee.

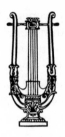

PART THE SECOND

And ye, sweet messengers, ye ninefold at
The ready ministration of your King,
I shall at long pore out mine eyes upon
This glancing main. How mightily it throws
At this bare, monumental pitch of rock
Whereon I stand! Years since, I put my muse
To reason's goodly school as, next the flame
That bows and dances o'er the scholar's lamp,
I spent away the careful hours of
My nonage. Hitherunto having bent
My plodding, philosophic way, by great
Divines and sages ever lit, I last
Attained to this commanding prospect of
The sea, the vast variety of all
That seems. Now, as I late was bold to breathe,
I wish, so it shall be to God becoming,
To lay a course below this dizzy steep
For Parnasse and those leaves that shine about
The brow beyond that fluid multitude.
    We painful heads will thrash and riddle from
Particularities their gen'ral truths,
Which when abstract beneath our bleaching gaze
Will want a savour and completeness. But
The Source of Truth, preventing hollow need
Has gently bidden divers men to lay
For all our starveling selves the feast of art.
From out th' innumerality that throngs
Upon our senses five, th' Almighty deigns
Such elements to fish as may be oned

To make a fable, strain, or comely shape,
Each in its kind reflecting His so brave
Creation—each an airy unity
Of gen'ral notion and particular
Example. All as in a ringing forge
These likenesses He roundly works as if
By hammerstroke and 'midst the answ'ring spill
Of candent sparks and showery flakes of fire.
This glowing handiwork, for men ordained,
To which, by grace, ye deftly ply your own
Creative hands, ye swiftly bear to those
Who wait at rest the sudden blaze of art.
Each semblance casts a fervid influence
That renders mortal mind and heart as flush
As fired steel and straight atones them in
A dazzling ecstasy. And so the Lord,
By playing fantasies on inward eye
And ear of artist intermedial,
To mankind gives that, like ye thunderlights
At intuition's stroke (who have, nor need,
Imagination), they should see and love
At once—should apprehend abiding truths
While corporate full in graceful blows of act
Or substance. Though such flow'rs be fictive shapes,
They own to mortal eyes more perfect or
More present symmetries reflecting His
Eternal Truth than e'er things unideal
May cede. And unto reason's work, which likes
Unto a moil of ants at prising of
The folded peony, those jealous flow'rs
And wry of actual creation do
But loathly yield their crabbed truths. And sure,
When discourse hales his prisoners abstract
To human gaze, they show them ghosts of wan
And stuffless kind. A tale exalt or touch
Of golden wires shall limn the Universe
More throughly than a lab'ring discourse or
A slate of formularies cramped. Than dull
Descriptions oils and marbles are more worth.

For art persuades the soul and toles her rapt
To everlasting life. Thus, perfect truths
Of visionary source alone beneath
The moon our blinkard understanding both
And promptly glad and breed. Oh, out of count
The number of His clemencies! How much
The scend of His beneficence, Who thus
Our souls with darts of joy will still traverse!
     Wherefore, ye streaming light of joy in truth,
I now unto my knees am fallen least
Of men to beg that in the torrent of
Your unremitting prayer ye would beseech
My Lord to send me by my Guardian true
The plotted charts of visionary tales
That unto humankind might character
The very world. And thou, my cherished Friend
And Minister, pray compass me about
When from this lofty brow of granite I
Shall urge my downward way and go amongst
My peers, who now discalced in whispered airs
And mild slow foot a many-dimpled trace
Upon the sodden verge of sand. They fare
From yond maternal harbour's gentle clasp,
Wherein they spent the golden light of this
Now silvering day in trimming everyone
His craft careened upon the dry and for
The near salt wave athirst. Myself, betimes,
Must slightly farther pilgrim to mine own
Dear craft beneath to brace her helm and scrape
Her crusted keel, to scan her cloth, and all
Her boatlong seams to pay full thick against
Their making water i' the tempest. When
I have dispatched these works and so thou shalt
Have brought that grace for which I e'vn now prayed
The Quires' high intercession, do thou deign
To hover o'er the mast and, as thou wast
A painted wind distent of cheek, bag forth
The beggar sails in crimson signed that soon
And long my prow of gaze serene might cleave

The panic of shouting foam and leaping waves
Upon the main. No Christian poet but
Avers that actions plotted down in tales
From Heav'n must have him scatheless to that leaved
And bloomy Mount of truths perennial.

    Remark now, Angel, how those bards go thence
To take their rest; they act as sure as gods.
(And so do I, I trow, thy little charge!)
Just so, I fancy, young Poseidon smoothed
And bridled the dolphin sea, fawning at
His sooth command. My ready watchman's glance
Flown forth this shore of my absorption shows
Me that the moon upon her mystic round
Has coaxed the shallows from their oozy bed.
But lo! what melancholy ruin is
Discovered to mine eyes? I barely make
Upon that mire the black remain of what
Was erst a worthy craft and sleek. How did
Her master helm her to this shape? Indeed,
I fear a shape delusory, if fair,
Was calved and made to witch his heart away
Until he drave upon a rock and quit
These wooden bones to worm and water. Oh,
Methinks I hear the beams cry out and split
Asunder! Oh, he casts him helpless on
The fluid mercies of the sea! 'Tis true
No bane will visit who shall wightly stand
Upon his course; but ere we poets young
Have squared the yards—before we yet have laid
Our noble tales abroad—we oft conceit
That we can breast the heaving ocean in
The cockle self-reliance and elude
The jagged mouths that lie agape beneath
The doubtful wave. Let all high-crested youth
Would fain strike o'er the surge bethink themselves
That, ere our eldest Parents fetched away
To wrack, that undersea extending far
Beyond the plummeting of mortal eyes
Was long the habitation of the bad.

O thou my Lamp celestial and all
Ye firmament of light, who condescend
To be our votive fires, ye know that these
Malign within the green abysm are
The very demonry disfellowed from
Your consort ages since. They count below
As many as the sumless grails that shroud
The beds of the interminable seas.
Ye also know that all this main is but
The welter of myself, and any self
Resolved as I to fetch the land beyond
The misty verge of straining human sight.
    In Greekish myth was blindly storied just
Such one as they that through these waters swim
To work destruction still. I speak of whom
Th' uncircumcised called Phorcus, him they might
Have named base sire of monsters; sea-god spawned
Of Hell; dim, diabolic libertine.
Now into dreadful Ceto, nearest of
His sib, he threw his wanton seed, whereat
She bulked prodigious as she swum the flood;
And like the schooling cows that crawl from out
The waves in spring, she last lay shuddering on
The strand and dropped a get of freaks that roamed
The frighted world and plagued the souls of men.
The cursed originals of Phorcus black,
Those more black moving in the deeps, still bend
Themselves to troll us shipmen from our course.
The poet's self, as any else's, would
To knowledge, pow'r, or mere sensation slave
Him, though he ne'er so gravely don the cap
Of manumission. But those Argus eyes,
His quiet lodgers, know that gladliest
He would but feel and verse his feelings to
The nerves of other men, for all he feed
Nor form will, intellect, or character,
Be they as shrinkshanks gone a begging with
The empty bowl. Thus, from the running throngs
That by his mind's five tributary locks

Attain his oceanic self, the fiends
Will seize perceptions apt and get upon
Them all such symbols or adventures as
Should answer his ignoble bent. No trope
Or action thus begot will ever show
Or story him the truth that he must go
Abroad himself and that along his gift
Of days, though he shall sometime federate
And sometime measure with the world externe,
'Tis sole above the wash he has his grace
And wends him fain to home and Father. Nay,
Like Ceto's whelp, Echidna, bold upon
The ocean, these perfidious calves of Hell
Will float all fair and sleek above the wave
Whilst coiling horrid all below it. How
So long the faring bard shall stand upon
His course, these monsters will lay wait for him
And rise like naiads from the glittering seas
About his keel that by impostures they
Might reach him from his high resolve and draw
Him heedless into a spangled shoal of dreams.
Therein, betimes, a spined and poisoned tail
In bubbling sweep may shard his skull, bestick
His heart, and send his headlong corse to ground
In midst the swirling nimbus of his blood.
      O Hosts on high, obtain for us stout bars
Of grace to make our souls all fast against
The mummery that yonder waits us. E'er
Before my sund'ring prow wave slow thy vans
In stately flight, my Guardian nigh; appall
Those thievish denizens below and look
Their miscreations back to Hell. Meseems
Thou urgest me to beg the ear of one
That lived, as I do yet, in flesh and time,
But one within the mountain's shadow of
Whose builded prodigies my deeds are as
The pebbled works and crimp thrown up of ants
Or eyeless moles. O sainted Thomas, child
Of Aquin, child of God, who now in sweet

Concent with angels descant far above
Th' eristic chirm of earth, incline those eyes
That nursed thy Herculean mind; observe,
Thou peer of the illuminating sun,
How parlous lies my road. I pray thee for
My speed ask fortitude of Him Who trod
Th' obedient sea and, swiftly quieting
The bully winds, drew Peter from the crowd
Of bumping waves. For that thy pow'rs informed
The flesh, thou wast of discourse straitly done
The emulated master. Who shall walk
The cobbles of thy narrow ways and walled
Will soon arrive the lucid square of truth.
      Wherefore, what hour forth sea or sky shall burst
The dazzling image in my sight—when loom
Unseen shall breathe a doing in mine ear
And press the bellied sail—do thou, my Saint
In everlasting orison, request
For me such craft of discourse as may teach
Me whether of the warring origins
The inspiration comes. From this self steep,
Which thou and other few of giant race
Did build aloft, those after issue of
The Stagirite and thee scanned hard the surge
And made three aberrations whereinto
Unhappy poets stray. The first, for all
Perhaps the least in Heaven's disesteem,
Is but the reinless use of threading wild
Abnormities and casualties rare,
The sugared cates that feed the tooth for bare,
Disjoint adventure—for the wonder of
Occurrences and deeds to which no likes
On earth were ever seen. Oh, what is time
If not God's stay of that great whetted blade
Upthrown to lay the human crop at length?
Within this spacious gift, He cites all things
To season in the mellow month and soft.
      This fullness whither He will ev'ry of
His creatures ripen, each in sev'ral kind

78

And unto sev'ral measure, is, in sooth,
The imitation of His glories. Now
Th' unfurlèd host of nature, oft of freak
And foil put by their course, but hint our eyes
The copious land to which they make. And thus
The part of him that o'er this heaving waste
Would ply the nimble pen in numbers is
To show in act the mimic tendency
That God bestows upon His creatures all —
Indeed, t'exhort the imitation of
His Christ. For man no matter urges save
Redemption. Hence, when minstrel's matter is
The truths that nearly bear upon our souls,
'Tis storying the flesh was giv'n a will
Unbound, who therewith shapes a course for good
Or bad, that fitliest avails us men
To grasp the bias of the golden world
And fetch the long felicity in Heav'n.
        The poet true will take the sea at float
And tell an action like and self-sufficed —
In train of cause and inevasible
Effect — that, when his boat he shall have banked
Afar, he shall this part of Augustine
Have bodied out: For God has moulded us
To be His own, our hearts shall have no rest
Until they wear their lengthful way to Him
And in the arms of His sweet lenity
Repose them like the prodigal returned.
O Thomas mine, near all whose thoughts would
        stand
Eternal law and full the famished clerk,
What wisdoms, what enlargements of the mind
Or soul has he that makes an idol of
The strange event and seldom? He will far
Extravagate through Faerie that from
The box he might e'er spring wry Jack. Along
An accidental roam of incidents,
He now perchance will have his hero to
A region lists and set him fierce at tilt

With headless knights, and now might give him o'er
To nerveless throes of passion for a may
Though he have neither seen nor spake her, but
Just spied her beauty's likeness brushed within
A locket's close. Though yielded it may be
That poets such will take the widow time
To wife and manly captain o'er the swells
To famous far the noble deed, as well
They might with keel but draw a circle on
The sea. For whiles they rove and touch upon
The many coasts of rare adventure, they
Forget or set at nought the poet's straight
And sacred purpose to the Mount Whose side
E'er pulses nectar to the parching tongue.
    Their talent dissipate in fleeting thrills,
They end at best by coyly harbouring
Where first they spread the spanking sail—no more
Percipient now than when they loosed for sea.
At worst, they end like rash Ulysses, who
Renounced the glowing hearthstone and with all
His ancient crew once more at bench and helm
Struck o'er the great, blind deep to find where he
Might graze the withered fruit that 'neath the Tree
Of Knowledge strow the dank, inhabited mould.
Upon a day, as they were sailing off
The wind a thousand leagues from charted tides,
A Mountain loomed upon their hungry stare;
And as they tilted nearer, frisking on
The little seas, there breathed a tempest forth
The slopes ahead that shortly span thrice round
The groaning ship, which by a whirlpit's maw
Was headlong gulfed, all hands aboard, their great
Incentor wild and clinging to a sheet.
    O thou that hammeredst iron proof against
The rams and bolts of error, fend us from
The second deviation witnessed by
Thy latter seed, who never stood this watch
But harmless and availed. Than errantries
Of knight fantastic—or he deftly play

The crimsoned axe or sweep the blushing lute—
This second wand'ring proves more arrant still,
Again more grave. The poet, weary of
The billowing way of action, will misprize
The grizel time; and, though he would not put
Her quite away, full oft he takes his leave
To seek the wanton moment's sooted eyes,
Her lips made shrill with paint. To passion he
Abandons him, as with his sorcerous tongue
He casts a glamour of infinity
About sensation; and, to spell away
The mind from very actualities,
He raises reveries unansw'rable
To reas'n or Heav'n's high Will. Thus robed around
With termlessness, the warrantable joys
Of recreation are upheaved upon
Inebrious shoulders and like strutting skins
Of wine are borne in lurching triumph to
A pantheon of follies, where upon
A pedestal they squat the idols of
An age. (Oh, vile and terrible to sight
Unsotted!) And, abjuring gen'ral truth,
The bard that would but feel must worship the
Particular—ere long, the fey: such things
As strange and fatal gleam. No longer does
He joy in fabling the sublimity
Of one inspirited in many; nay,
He only loves to verse the sev'ralty
Of things, nor will he deign to own therein
The unity, how large so'er it loom
Throughout. Ere long, he gratulates himself
As one so keenly passible as scarce
To be assorted with the kind of man.
The more abnormous the emotions of
This sagging jack-afloat, the quicklier
From battled poop he flourishes them to
The soapless multitude of normal breed
He scorns but unto whom will posture ay.
Sweet sun and saint, whose fame will tell what years

Remain this world, no bard shapes true his course,
Though he should sail the farthest seas of earth,
But stays within the homely wick of men.
Pray speed, O Lord, the faithful poet's clean
And ever-flying timber unto Thee!

    But cast a princely sight once more, great Saint
At such a bard as mads for sentience.
In search of ecstasies he rides from isle
To shimmering isle, each one unwonted more
And further witched than that he rummaged last.
Not long his ship may gently heave and set
At anchor ere upon the ocean line
Must glimpse that fat avernal grandly hight
Satiety, who lepers all delight
And pirates all this poet's treasured hopes.
The victim, letting groans and walling round
His eyes, once more makes sail to gain from his
Tormenter and another Lotus-Land
Invent. So far he wanders from the course
He charted first that ev'ry normal thing
He glances, ev'ry the sublimest and
The least, stands fair to touch him piteously
Upon the raw. Thus ever deeper bores
The maggot in this poet's musèd brain.

    The colourable objects of his quest
Are diversly th' Almighty, brotherhood,
The transcendental she (this latter if
His tide of humours flood to womanwards),
And, last, the woodlands wild. Communion all
Without himself he wants; but God for him
Is only immanent—but dwells within
The fabric of His vast creation, as
He were Himself a creature. And the vast
This poet gazes pales no object, for
His dogged fancy crowds it full with all
His woolly reveries and wishes, all
Which batten ruthlessly and graze it clean.
The universe is victuals to a sheep.
In fine, he is himself his universe;

His god is but himself. What need of grace?
Himself of kind is graced. Is not his heart
With sentiment awash? If haply reas'n
Or will he want, in russet liv'ry of
His dreams obsequious they wait.
                                    Now in
His soft Arcadian strain, he ofttimes sings
The brotherhood of Man, a creature of
His civic mood, a phasm quaintly like
Himself, impatient of such remoras
As venerable use and weariful
Moralities that dare to urge upon
A throbbing exquisite the carlishness
Of self-denial. Who, dear Saint, will not
Upon the stony way drag up and bear
The splint'ry burthen of his cross not long
Will keep his yielding heart from growing stark
As stone and last will hardly deign to draw
The merest sliver out his neighbour's quick.
And though this Perigot shall set his flock
A-bleat upon the passing gladness of
Fraternity and through his oat shall flute
Hortations to the world how they must to
Their feeling breasts their reeds accord and straight
An universal diapason breathe
Of brother's love, there follows straight in sad
Reality such scrannel din as should
All eared creation vex and harrow. Nought
There is so private and respective as
The heart, withal so vagrant. Wherefore how,
Thou burning phare, shall scattered be enleagued,
Or how conventional eccentric? Thence
Recoiling each from other in a harsh
Disownment, some through wild of Arcady
Will maze in several and gather wool
From wiry bramble, where their frighted dreams
And silly now seek refuge. Other some
That in the name of fair fraternity
Struck off their fathers' heads and rolled them 'neath

83

A trampling multitude of cattle fall
At strife among themselves — pull Phrygian caps
In mutual suspicion — till at length
A wily Hobbinol and mighty shall
Outtop his black-browed fellows and require
How they his brothers now must be or paint
Their crimson life upon his new-beat sword,
On which his governance to serve they smart
Bestow a kiss, in all fraternity.
  Near all such poets of this scatt'ring as
To dalliance propend conceit, each one,
A vap'rous nymph that leads his cap'ring heart
A pretty dance. In blue beyond his reach,
She glints the void intaglio of his dreams,
Whereof on earth no waxen woman can
He find t'accept the fair impression. Yet
Her planetary eyes keep ever quick
The livid flame within his breast. Between
Two deeps of blue the poet steers: above
His sail still smiles the high serene; beneath
The plowing strakes the hungry gulf still yawns.
O Patron blissfully at praise within
The bastion of God, who ne'er so nice
The plumb and level of thy reason pliedst
As when with Blood of the Incarnate Word
Thou here becam'st inebriate, pray, an
Th' All Knowing it shall like, incline and by
A still locution ask the poet spelled
Of wafting nymph if he can say from which
Cerulean burn the lucent eyes he stares.
His slippery heart has stroked and lullabied
His poppied wits to sleep, and now he weens
That upward bend his thirsting orbs to catch
The streams of Heaven's slaking influence.
In sorry sooth, he o'er the gunwale bends
His length to gaze the eyes that beckon 'neath
Th' abysm's lifting verge until with feet
In air he librates o'er perdition like
A giddy child. Whilst thus he drifts, he far

Outsheers his elder precedent, who will
Indeed conceive a mistress for his knight,
But thrones her as a stainless damozel
Within a star-enwreathèd tow'r that by
Celestial filaments enlaced she might,
If blithely, heave her plated gallant as
A beetling lobster off the carnal ground
Of life. And so was trothless sense bound o'er
As handmaid unto spirit's airy sway.
    But spirit, all adust, is now haled down
In chains and chatteled 'neath the mired heel
Of sense grown insolent. As often as
This later bard shall gather to his breast
A rosy may that sweetly minds him of
His smiling dream, he sings her as the glass
Of translunary good, the mirror of
His feeling soul. He trills her thus till her
Inevitable kidney or her own
Chimera intervenes for thorns to show
Her weary and unworthy of his heed.
O browsick he! betrayed to mis'ry by
His spectral fair, who softly laughs and fleets
Away, nor long omits to beckon. Or
In cold adieu he lip the hectic cheek
Of love despised, or in a fiery pique
His blistered front from scorn redeem, he casts
Away, as 'twere perforce, that he might find
His dream aflash within the dimpling pools
Of still another earthly maiden's eyes.
    And so, twice, thrice, and more he shall relive
This Cupid's tale until his wasting hopes
Once cordial shall languish throughly pricked
And bled, as pig-like he will needs swill down
The brimming stoup of flat futility.
And ne'er the She whose love he fondly hopes
Was in the smallest wise what bonny one
Of frame and soul drew living breath before
Him. Nay, and who than thou more swiftly sees
Consociate of angels, that the She

This poet weeps and sings will prove upon
A closer eye to be in very deed
His greedy self, all farded, veiled, and coy.
    At pains to ward the darts of ridicule
An histrionic pose he strikes amidst
The palace fall'n about his crimson ears.
And though the heart of whom he loved, and leaves,
Shall be opprest with shame or love unpaid,
Yet hardly can the humble thought engage
His mind to do for her avail, ne e'en
Put up for her a moment's pray'r: but he
Must wrap him in the weeds of woe; have done
With faithless humankind; and, bidding all
A frigid valediction, stalk away
To join those kithless and unfathered souls
That cloistered them within the hollow wild
The phantom wool to pluck. For now he would
Commune with that wherein it pleases them
To box the vasty name of Nature, e'vn
The stolid hosts of hills and trees, which prove
Betimes but cold to men and rooted fast
In unrelenting fealty to God.
    By sophistries and crooling song, he sends
The pickets of his heart and soul to sleep;
And though sometime he goes at large as on
His nimble four to bell his passions like
A fervid brute, he oftener reclines
To vegetate in golden reveries
With bushes. Thus, he holds himself for wise.
Not maidens now, who want a pliancy
Of will and intellect, but cataracts
Allure and thistledown compels, which will
Become as hinds to be in spirit rent
And eaten by a pride of metaphors.
What need to say to thee, thou sovran mind
In God secure, that not with boscage or
The writhen rock does this forlorn commune:
He does but congress with his tangled moods,
Admire as in a glass the crumbling chalk

86

That idly postures for a monument.
　　As go the lives of men, no matter or
These votaries of feeling shall declare
For God or man or nymph or nature, they
Near ev'ry quivering sentient will in time
And all upon a sudden fetch aground
Before a restive barren of regret.
Sensation is the transcendental goal,
So strangely, so vertiginously felt
That eye should hear the setting sun, as if
The little conchs of mortal listening
Might catch Hyperion jolting to the verge
On rumbling wheels; that through the hours of ev'n
No poet's nose that shall inspire above
An open phial of attar but should look
The reeling song of ruddy-petalled flow'rs
Or keenly feel the booming humble-bee
About his furious and civic task;
That ear, engulfed alike, should weirdly eye
Sweet Progne's twittered arabesques and eft
Upon the breathless night the storied web
Of Philomela's mystic jargoning;
That tongue should smack the Muse's twang of wire
Or taste the feeble shriek of dainties milled
Between the clashing regiments of teeth.
(Thus, fain is ev'ry vatic bard of sense
Transcendent to be rid of storied deeds—
Of ev'ry whiff and peep of agency
That might his scarebabe, fell Ponderiact,
Arouse, who blames him for a craven and
A Sybarite whose duties all disowned
Are scarce the less to do.)
　　　　　　　　But though a bard
Upon the main shall peer both long and prone
For raptures, he will ween in rue how full
As long as he shall run right stoutly buoyed
This side the veil of dissolution he
May never hope to word or e'en perchance
Be sensible of these obscure delights

Stirred to and mingled as with witch's wand,
All which thereat he hazards to account
Among the everlasting guerdons of
A blest eternity, as if the Lord
In mockery stood ready to bestow
Upon th' Elect the stone, the scorpion, of
A vulgar riot for their portion. Thou
Whose dow'r of mind was dawn to sunless souls
And whose much sanctity was noon, this gull
Assevers that his goal is Heaven high,
But surely 'tis himself. He longs, in truth,
T'include him fast within the closet of
His innest gaudy dreams and, like a tame
And bloodless cageling, nightly warble e'en
The substance of his minglements and moods
To ears beyond the veil that billows forth
His casement dark. To spell one's fellow men
This wise, howe'er, there needs a gramarye
The like whereof this bard has ne'er so much
As thought; and thus, although he would maroon
His sweating oar, slave discourse still misprized,
He needs must flog him into pulling through
An explanation lucid and direct
Of all those turbid synaesthetic joys
To be beyond this weary burgher's tale
Of earthly tedium. 'Twere better far
To put a nobler charge upon abused
Discursion, who besteads his master best
When he is bid to sweep the staring prow
Dead through a plotted trial of worthies, whose
Inweaving intercourse twixt swaddling bands
And winding sheet tries good from ill and soon
Describes in high-wrought web and many-hued
The very front of universal Truth,
Whose gaze serene gives men to quiet mind.
    Grown faint with duteously laying on
The bloody lash, which only feebles whom
It urges on, the jaded bard has waxed
Impatient of eternity and to

The whisp'ring strand near which he lately came
Aground he lends a languid eye; for might
Not here, he thinks, be haply found a means
The masterly avail of which should from
The irksome, explicative round of pull
And glide abstract his spleeny self, so keen
To roll in boundless multitude? But more
By much, he aches to verse in ev'ry of
His kindred ears as veninous a brew
Of moods inebriant as ever sod
Within an iron heart. A pregnant while
He poises what to do; and then, with hope
That he should light at last upon his legs,
From off his timber's edge he leaps and lights
Upon the sand. Scarce inland has he trod
Beyond the sea-beat yards when straight there strikes
His dazzling eyes a radiant form come nigh.
It is the Lady Circe, and the isle
His tousled bark has lurched upon is just
That Aea, seat of all her doings fey,
Whence bards set forth upon the desperate third
Of those three errancies thine issue named.
    With blandishments and graceful becks, she has
Him to her tower. Stupidly, he goes
Much like those sacrificial bulls of yore
Ringed, wreathed, and ponderously biddable
To blood-washed altars builded to appease
The gods of Hell. Now Circe, comliest
Of timeless hags and ancient minion of
The angels damned, by witchwork would become
This poet's evil muse. Right soon he tells
His tedium and sighs his dearest wish,
The twain to her well-known or e'er he spake.
In soothful flow of words, she prays him to
Repose his misery in her and speaks
That he shall have his heart's long hope within
That glooming, bluer deep that hissed before
His sev'ring prow but gaily flashes in
Presentiment upon his mudded keel.

Now warming to her work, she plies him thus:
Such sophic heads as he know how that vast
Of blue aloft, suffused and flooded with
The ever-streaming brilliance of the sun,
Could hardly be the haunt to which he shows
Him naturally fain. Indeed, t'embrace
The wild'ring, dizzy joys he craves, he need
Not wait the fearful-singing blade that strews
The bent and bearded harvest flat. This side
The waxen shroud, his goal is hard at hand
In Ocean's deep and murk delights of mood
And synaesthetic gurging. See, thou Saint,
Who wardest well thy suppliants' reasonings
Till Heaven's orbs and crosses round their minds,
How now this flatt'ring coz'ner twines him with
Her sophistry, which draws and cumbers like
That boneless fish whose suckered arms grow forth
A soft and bagging head. In fine, she vows
That peace eludes him that he yet retains
His weariful drudge, discursion and, great shame
To say, indites as he were dragged e'en now
At imitation's florid wheel, which bears
The brazen car of tyranny and runs
The lyric fair of self-evincement o'er,
The stoic world whereat by grief at last
Undone at loss of this Melpomene's
So intimate, withal so instantly
And widely warbled lay. But he turn out
His oar and greasy turnspit, quite refuse
To mount the wearing tumult of the sea,
And sink beneath the billows blue, he ne'er
Shall have his happiness, which sole within
The sweet enfoldments of that deep-laid port
Of joy may be possessed. More nimble than
Arachne bold, she weaves her tissue of
Vermillion philosophic lies dropt o'er
With golden flatteries, a standard brave
Yet one beneath the streaming insolence
Of which the breathless poet somewhat fears

T'enlist his easy shame. Perceiving then
The ague of a moment's fear hunt out
His newly covert heart, she makes a smile
Behind which she convenes her inward pow'rs.
She bears to be his only friend, to word
Her simple heart, and this all only for
His good. Would he, a cavalier of fame,
Decline to put his fellow suitors to
The blush? And like the fabled fox, would he
Then slink inglorious away the while
Protesting that the scented bays by muse
Enwreathed to grace the Orphic brow are but
A sere and cankered mat of weeds? Not long
May souls as finely sensible as he
Ignore desires they know cannot be reined.
He would demean him ill in trepidly
Abridging him of aught that goes to make
Him throughly self-apaid. Thus, whenso he
Shall hear the far sirenic notes at play
Upon the lightsome gales, Oh, let him fend
The hands of his too-ready servant reas'n,
That meddling oar, who would his master's ears
Estop and straitly lash him to the mast!
The deeps of self the poet must descend;
But ere he shall implunge with silver shoals
To antic, he shall have of her a wand
Of wizard pow'r wherewith in poesy
To bear a god's dominion over all.
    So on she earwigs deeper still a hatch
Of further lies to lay that they might reel
The balance of his wheedled mind till it
Should lowly stoop to her. With warmth she vows
How first his sigil grandly sweeping, he
Will equal man and worm and star and weed.
In fancy thus declaring all the world
To be a fluid heap of sand, a dust
Of atoms 'neath his spirit's awful tread,
He will his senses' five great bartizans
Embattle, whence like Rhenish brigands he

Might spoil at will the passing argosy
Of treasures to his purpose. Draining forth
The upward orb of boist'rous doing, they
Will through the narrows to the downward orb
Of lang'rous musing droop. Thence farther will
They plummet, through the lowest nethers of
His soul, until the very ground of his
Unreason they shall heap, where swim just off
The phosphorous slime the shapes of nameless dreams.
    'Tis of his poet's mystery, she lips,
To give these swimming dreams, say rather moods,
A tenancy within these looted pearls,
Which thus possessed and by their tenants warped
Fair out of countenance are then become
The very stuff of poesy, what things
May emblem and imply to fellow hearts
Those synaesthetic states that chastely bloom
As long as he shall make his soul's stout door
Full fast against the shameless bravery
Of time. And she will lift the burthen of
Composing from his bended shoulders, where
Rough reason plumped it down as if upon
A blinkered beast before he urged him o'er
The waste with thumpings of his iron rod.
    For now no more is here to do than from
The drunken pen quite hazardously to
Asperse the vacant page with mystic glyphs,
To make a heavenscape of revery
That may bedew the parching world beneath
With fatal influence. Mispainting thus
With oily versatility, she worms
Yet farther 'cross the front of truth to tell
Him how in numbers thus appearing he
Shall be to angels liked, e'vn that great host
In fires of refusal still aswim,
A battle casqued and sharply horrid yet —
But delicately pensive therewithal —
Who scorned to look the blinding Tyranny
That thrones Him in the apse of Heav'n and hence

Betray themselves so proudly gripple of
Their inward galaxies of forms innate,
The glinting coins of intellection true
And instant, all without the plane of time.
And if his noble moods shall want somewhen
An intuition's iron consonance
With fact, the sheer intensity of his
Poetic constellations shall upheave
A fierce, titanic bore that shall upon
Its monstrous shoulders bear him hurtless through
The grinding narrows of ungenerous
Reality. (Oh, most egregious lie!)
    For that he came within this world a gross
Extrusion from the void and void within
Of those ideas wherewithal the sheer
Created spirits had been found, he must,
'Tis roundly claimed, to prove the worth of that
His fancy may invent take counsel with
His reason. Here her orbits look as set
With living coals, such eyes as beaming from
The Aegis might have stared the world to stone.
She shrills how reason is a grimy shroff
That twixt his teeth delights a dream new struck
To bend and show it for an obolus
Would hardly have a blackguard's soul across
The livid flow of Styx. No right has reas'n,
She vows, to hobble Pegasus though sprung
From monstrous blood, for throbbing art may not
Be stilled. Thus, breathing feeble arguments
As they were fire, she tells her bard right out
That he must never reck the morrow, no
Nor grave monition said alow within
His heart. Before aught else he must not hold
Him unto aught responsible. He must
Reject all things would impudently put
A fealty upon him. 'Tis but he,
She hoos, must be the monarch of his soul.
    And now, dear Guide, she fancies that she hears
Just off the summit of her vap'rous head

93

The rustling wings of Victory with bays
In hand her brow to bind. The poet now
Shows suasible to any urgency
She fain would speak. And thus, in clamant tones
That cite the pulsion of his blood, she bids
Him to his boat again, which gently rolls
Upon an evening tide becrimsoned of
The dying sun. He must embark, spread sail,
And run until beneath his keel shall gape
The ocean's boundless deep, o'er which arrived
He will at once forsake his ancient prore
And all the nuisance of her gnarlèd ropes
And ritual (what feeling soul could long
Remain her master?) and will slip for ay
And o beneath the darksome swells. This last
Of her malarias exhaled, he hastes
Away her urgent will to work as he
By barking terriers were chased. Ere long,
Above the gulf he rides the tossing deck
Once more, but rides forgetful of the boat
That bears him up, her hold of noble words
And numbers neat, and heedless how in long
Despite of naiads, spouts, and sea-drakes she
Once fastly bare him dry and homewards o'er
Old Ocean's hugely rolling sinews. Now
Uncordial to any gale would hie
Him on, he furls and in a wanton rite
Of malice breaks th' unfeigning sail stone with
His warping wand. At once he drops beshrewed
And like a boulder through the fluent veil
To dwell where dungeoned madness grins amidst
The shrouding legions of the dead and damned.
    O Thomas glad, thou beaming ruby blushed
Of God's sweet ravishing, ye angels blest,
Bright diamonds whose ev'ry face afire
At once retains and still to God returns
Its sev'ral beam of fervid blessedness
Come forth the furnace of His infinite
Completeness, prithee ask a grace of Him

Whom all we love (though I a sinner yet)
That might this poet gently mesh and rap
Clean out the ruthless, breathless sea of self.
    But thou, O region angel here beneath,
The guardian of this lost to view, as lost
To grace, meseems in prompt obedience to
Divine decree, thou frownest now; for lo,
The welkin beetles o'er with sudden cloud
That sables all the main. And sure thy breath
It is that yonder stirs the shivering waste.
O saints and hallowed quires on high, behold
A funnelled, fatal cloud in awful gyre
Descending as it were a finger of
Th' Omnipotent! Whilst rooted in the pall
That streams above, it lights in furious spin
Upon the dreadful sea and scours forth
Inscribing "Havoc" on the tortured waves.
From out this roaring tongue of wind, within
The course this airy stylus now describes,
Methinks I hear and read the sturdy kind
Of praise it soon will render up to God's
Omnipotence. It makes direct for that
O'erclouded rag of sand, proud Circe's haunt,
Erewhile deliriously shimmering i'
The flaming air. Its mistress high upon
Her stony keep, descries th' approaching harm.
Though inly stunned she gloriously makes
As if she had it in contempt. But now
Her liver quails within the gripe of fear,
And she recourses unto desp'rate plaints
And curses dire. Behold the storm with all
Its nameless terrors hard upon her. She
Would play the gorgeous heroine and clutch
A writhing aspic to her milken breast.
O fie upon pretense! With bloody nails
She flays her cheeks and howls her panic grief
At Heav'n, which herewith bears to this accurst
The deadly issue of her labours. Full
Upon the isle, the wrackful pillar moves;

Though late it gathered up the frantic swells,
It now uptears a whirl of biting rock
And sand, wherewith accoutred cap-a-pie
It coils the tower round in fierce embrace
And looses ev'ry mortared stone. In brief
Relentment, lo, it suffers all the pile
To drop unstrung upon the gasping earth!
    Now even as the fabric nodded to
Its thund'rous fall, the whilom chastelaine
Was borne distract amongst the horrors of
The welter's upward drafts, wherein she makes
Such shrieks as sole the tempest's mightful throat
Can dumb. Immit, O Saint and angels, yet
Another prodigy: At ev'ry mouth
And angry grin wherewith she wries her face
Erst fair, she moulds without advertency
A new and hideous front that squarely charts
Her deep-laid villainies; the fleets of tears
She streams her rose-, nay blood-dyed cheeks withal
Engrave in jagged, ever-during wakes
The vagrant courses of her greedy gulls.
And wheresoe'er her victims unto death
Implunged appears a fiery pock. Above
The anger sedulously furrowing
Her brow, the locks entwine in motion wrought
Of more than urgent wind; for see, they change
By one and one to flickering vipers, which
Now one, now other drop the head to sting
The face of who without all bowels lured
Unhappy men to Hell. Now blown aslant
The boist'rous, terror-breathing night, she hurls
To seaward like a thunderstone and through
The surges bowls, O holy ones, as if
From cannon's maw she had been vomited
Ahead a blust'rous rout of writhing flame.
    The tutelary vicar of these skies
Serenely curbs his snorting meteors
Of fire and deluge and, relaxing all
The whirlblast's twisted sinew, hies away

96

The silent herd of cloud. Quite gone that old
And awless jade that ever lessened grace
In men and poesy and must with long,
Incogitable pangs once pay within
The cold for-ever of perdition. Now,
This vision flown, though scarce to be forgot,
Mine eyes the clear, discovered sky survey,
Vast floors of deepest dye besprent across
With living gems as from most princely Hand.
To me they show as symbols of yourselves;
As, shining o'er the waters strown and still,
They smile me out of fear and eager to
Be down and set upon the main to tell,
As well to live, the course of martyrdom
And glory far above the poet shrined
Within himself, a rigid corpse entombed.
　　But look you! the approaching lord of day
Begins as with a seep of woad to hue
And clarify the eastern night; and though,
In turn, the many-schooling stars begin
Like dolphins blithe and debonair to sound
Within this tiding blue of morn, one Star
In undiminished oriency shines
Just o'er the golden nimbus of the dawn.
More pure, more bright she beams than ever shone
The brightest of those flames that yonder bow
And through the purpled arras take their leave.
Indeed, ye interceding gods, since that
Becrimsoned shut of yestere'en, no star,
Methinks, has shone till now. By grace of God,
This far yet hugely coruscating fire
Cites not my heart to wonderment, which oft
A gaping innocency will pretend
Whilst in the tickling, agitable soul
It plies the thistle curiosity
To evil purpose. Nay, within this breast
Her influential beams a holy awe
Inspire, the seed of sweet humility.
　　Whatever mingled exhalations of

My waking nerves may rise, I would not set
Them running up the sky like spectral beasts
Of earth to ravish and possess a star,
Which thus become an emblem twisted of
My vanity must meanly hobble in
A clubfoot row of numbers. Rather am
I fain to like this morning lamp unto
That pure mosaic gaze that shows within
The golden air aglitter high above
The altars of Byzantium. Dear my Saint
And angels aerial, to me this fire
Of purity may fitly emblem One
That dwells an infinite remove from all
My lowness, One withal the Crucified
Ere forth He breathed His sacred soul to God
His Father, gave (oh, gift unhoped!) for mine
Own Mother mild. O Mary, burning heart
And pierced, who beaconest the toiling prows
That crawl the surly seas across the port
Of God to scry, O heart that shin'st above
The gladsome, circling quires that sing Thee Queen
Of all creation, haste, I pray, Thine ear
Of grace t'incline to me, confiding how
Though sure I kneel this morn Thy meanest child
Thou'lt hear and help as ay. The lightening hour
Is come wherein, so grant Thy Son, in calm
Expectance I shall pick my downward way
(Right heedfully lest the balm should spill that brimmed
This brittle phial my heart along my wake
Of pray'r). When next shall flood the cove beneath,
Which slumbers still and dreams, I ween, the gests
And hazards high of youth, I would upon
My timber's deck the hempen fingers of
The harbour's sleepy ward be casting off
And heaving forth a sail to meet the airs
Of aureate morn. O blessed Cynosure!
The Guide at once and Inspiration of
Thy poets' hearts, when yet a little I
Shall loose for sea 'twill be Thy radiance bids

Me forth to meet my God across this gulf
And sweeping flood of dreams and deeds. O see
Above the earth's red rim he hugely springs,
The symbol of Thy Son, the Christ of God,
And closes ev'ry eastward-gazing eye
With instant awe this Easter of the day!
My hand as e'er in Thine, sweet Mother of
My bursting heart, I prithee lead me down
And gently to my going hence to reach
The harbour of my Saviour's opened Side.
    And thorough all my careful days upon
The wayward blue pray send me towardly gales
Of inspiration and the grace to keep
A poet's present hand upon the wheel,
To keep the symmetry and rhythm of
A course that may in numbers body forth
To men the glorious tragedy of one
That dies to self as highest Love brings down
The peen of grace upon the metal of
His firèd soul with love and martyrdom
Candescent. Whilst I sail the heaving waste —
That blear and fishful sea — pray scatter all
The shining tribes that promise hurt. Thou know'st
One side my way will loom grey Scylla, she
The bard o'ernice mishallows for the One,
The rock of gen'ral truth — for men, how all
Their happiness is found imbosomed in
The sweet convention of their wills with God's
Illuminous Mind. Upon a doleful day
Great ages since, that Circe that a trice
Ago was helped to fetch a timely leap
To seawards of the tempest's roar was spurned
By Glaucus, who to Scylla was more true
Than sailstone to the Pole, for which despite
Not Glaucus but th' unhappy Scylla bare
The witch's greenest hate. Fell Circe weaved
An evil word and stirred it full within
The waves in which fair Scylla oft beguiled
The scorching hours of afternoon. Ere long,

Then, Scylla bathed as she was wont and whilst
Disporting found her sprouting forth a zone
Of monstrous heads. Thus hideously spoiled
She rose in single, monumental dread
And loathing, whereupon she turned into
A cape of stone, from thence to stand a tomb
Of fear and port for ev'ry pavid bard
Whose blood within him clings do he but ween
Unwonted stir beneath the tireless pomp
Of ocean. Thus above the waters she
Has loured ever eft, say, rather, o'er
The toils; and oft she muses how they quite
Enough had done had they no more than buoyed
And cooled her sweltered limbs — when yet a limb
She owned. These flowing toils, to usher on
My argument, dear Mother, are a strait
In which hard by the bank opposing whirls
Charybdis, cleped as well the Many, eye
Of Ocean, where the treble errancies
Abide whereof I late bespoke and long
Th' angelic Thomas. Round this reeling pit
They madly foot a tarantelle to which
They bid all poets passing nigh, the wise
Of whom this invitation spurn and with
An equipoise of mind their course to God
Maintain. Alas, that coward crew forespoke,
Poor pidgeonhearts, oft stand too much in fear
Of coming nigh Charybdis. Like a fox
In eggs, dismay their mettle mouths in shards
And takes the worthy lap of their resolve.
    It longs to him would come most near the sun
To call such gentles forth the fiery air
As in a stately dance of doings may
Display the One of universal truth
Become embodied in the Many. Hence,
No course is his but that he pained his mind
To chart before he stood away from port
To track his foaming way the vast of blue
Across, nor boldly bearing off from his

Career to foot it with the treble fiends
Beneath—in impious despisal of
The One, nor canting off in terror that
The Many morrice all too nigh, but, like
An arrow, sailing all between and thus
Inerrably to Christ, the archetype
Of ev'ry worthy tale, or sad or blithe.
    Upon such day as offers high revolt
Against a generation's weary use
Of welt'ring with the nereids three within
The watery gyre, it tides not rarely that
A bard by fashion mewed but puts away
For Scylla's frowning heights, which, when he fetch,
A vengeance falls him sore as swift. While yet
He closes with her granite flank, behold!
From forth an antre sighing pestilence
A grisly drake its stone-eyed head protends
And grinning beastlywise invades the boat.
With holders flashing in its reeking jaws,
It rapes him from the deck and casts him down
At length upon the iron strand. In voice
That bleeds his ears the monster booms how he
Must ever cast his troubles on its care,
How, whenso he shall ply the glinting flood,
He must great Scylla coast, nor never draw
Aught nearer to Charybdis, coiling and
Voracious, than the flowing purlieus hard
Along the base of Scylla's frozen stare.
At once the poet vows away his will
And gladly hears as from an oracle
How he must put that mistress of deceit,
Proud-mind imagination, to the ban;
For she, oh make no doubt, was ever leagued
With those three limbs of Satan swimming yond
Within the wreathing waters, where they quire
To ev'ry bard that passes nigh their fair
Mendacities, their amiable lies.
    In accents that announce the pedant, the
Appalling worm assevers how there sole

Requires a method wherewithal the bard
May sing the universal all without
Imagination's rage and fury. Here
The slavering beast, which joyed of yore to foul
Bright Scylla's bloom, a dusty treatise puts
Upon the bard, within the crowding leaves
Whereof are charactered in close array
A regiment of rules, the myrmidons
Of regularity. He hears that when
He shall have schooled him in these canons, he
Shall verse and stave build high by hurtling dint
Of cold mechanic skill, without so much
A puff of troublous inspiration as
Should stir the down of eaglet's wing. If I
May instance Thee a rule that in the eye
By Scylla awed looms far more terrible,
O cause of all our joy, than any else,
One dare not ripened nature imitate
Direct. The poet must recourse instead
To paradigms, to wit, those bards of eld
That burst upon the buoyant wing and scaled
The heights of morn till, planing on the breath
Of angels through the vasts above, they looked
Upon the noontide blaze of heaven. Now
No doubt can be how th' imitation of
Such spirits by the fledgling bard both meet
And furthersome has been so it have made
Him love the truth and have so far from damped
His inward fires of high conceit as it
Should fan them brighter still. Thou knowest well,
Who tak'st the humbled bard to mercy, that
This narrow-heart of scales and coils will wreak
This rule upon its staring toy that he
Should still keep cold his forge and dark. For should
He set himself to glass direct the full
Accomplishment that nature purposes,
Though ever only hints to mortal heads,
He needs must court the fructifying airs
Of inspiration. Such audacity

His bilious lord will never stomach, for
Its bloodless charge might feel the spoom of mad
Charybdis and disturb his hearers with
A word or do unguessed. The poet quelled
Must coolly fall a-copying the books
Of all his betters. He must prise the lids
Of coffers not his own and thence abstract
A diction and fair poetries of myth
That, if his mind shall nothing forgetive
Or aught deep-going be, that is, shall be
A faithful liege to Scylla, he will but
Employ for pretty ornaments to trick
The tedium of his muse-forsaken verse.

     O Thou that trod'st and crushèd'st th' insinuant brow
Of writhing Hell, what lies has Satan left
Unhissed within the ears of men? This drake,
An image of his own tyrannic self,
Is certes e'en that blood-eyed fee-faw-fum,
A conscience miscreate, which he will put
As hard on wretches kindly finikin
As on such bards as dread all multitude
And motion of the sea. 'Tis true as sad
How flush imagination given o'er
To its devices to Charybdis will
Recourse and riot with the fuddlecaps
That reel therein. But by one beaming drop
Of the illimitable deep of grace
That flooded forth Thy Son's most holy Wounds,
Imagination shall be throughly cleansed
And, riding sure upon the shoulder of
That orbèd tide, be to the middest clime
Conveyed of Ocean's race twixt rock and gurge,
Upon which midsea reason's timber shall
Abide so it shall be, in happy turn,
Pressed gently thither fore a mist of grace
By Thee aspersed. Imagination to
The midst attaining, reas'n shall bring her straight
To wife and, following the roister of
The merry dolphins, to the leavy Side

That hangs above the orient reaches of
The wave. Their issue will be poems of
A man, to time, the scroll 'neath reason's quill,
Both wived and true, nor feigning timeless pow'r
Of seizing fast a fiery sooth as swift
As e'er an angel writes a levin bolt
Across the sky, no tale or discourse gone
Before. To none but spirits pure belongs
This pow'r of intuition, strung with all
Its airy, easy sinew. As all minds
By Heaven had to wisdom understand,
The intuitions that the bard of sense
O'erfine makes arrogant to call a grasp
Of truth, as they were e'en the noonlight of
Angelic intellection, are but blind
Sensation tasted o' the sudden and
In thorough want of concord with the real.

O fairest Flow'r of Heaven's hue, O real
And never feigning, whom I whisper beads
Of love and obsecration rathe and late,
Herewith I drop swift steps to strand and sea.
An humble birth, to Him I follow Thee.

MASTER NICHOLAS
CONTRA MUNDUM

Since Christendom with pocks of heresy
O'erspread—th' infernal Maggot batt'ning on
Its heart—hath fall'n at heavy length to dree
A scourge of cank'rous chastisement, how, John,
Shall thy begotten Nicholas abide,
Who once must quit thy gates to crawl below
That gnostic eye and old upreared in pride
And quick with ill as th' living gleeds that strow
The marl of Hell? Tho' thou and Anne above
Your darling wake more fierce than e'er that dam
That suckled infant Rome, how may your love
Ensteel him? Lo, I need but word this sham
Of thought to hear its hollow faith; Who thwarts
Th' red Worm can headlong pride as it were orts.